Cycling
East Michigan

30 Of The Best
Bike Routes In
East Michigan

Cycling
East Michigan

30 Of The Best
Bike Routes In
East Michigan

By Karen Gentry

Published by Thunder Bay Press
Production and design by Pegg Legg Publications
Maps by Michele Miller, Miller Design, Grand Rapids
Editing by Wally Palazzolo
Printing by Eerdmans Printing Company, Grand Rapids,
Michigan
Cover Photo by Karen Gentry
Inside photography by Karen Gentry and Jim DuFresne
unless otherwise noted.

ISBN: 1-882376-12-9

Printed in the United States of America

96 97 98 99   2 3 4 5 6 7 8

Lansing, Michigan

Two cyclists take in the view of Wild Fowl Bay at the end of Crescent Beach Road in the Thumb of Michigan.

An invitation...

From the rocky shores of Wild Fowl Bay to Ann Arbor's Huron River,

Along the Grand and Red Cedar on the River Trail,

Through the campuses of MSU and CMU,

Follow the awesome AuSable, view Great Lakes lighthouses,

Circle motorless Mackinac Island,

Journey across covered bridges and over the "Tridge" in Midland,

Come and discover with your bicycle the byways, backroads and bike trails of East Michigan.

k.g.

30 BICYCLE TOURS IN EAST MICHIGAN

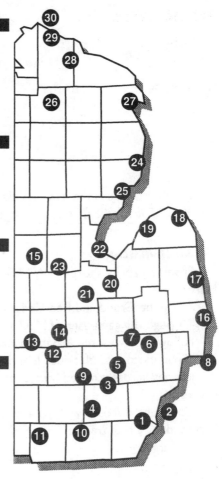

Contents

Acknowledgments

Whew! What a ride it's been.

When *Cycling Michigan: 25 of the Best Bike Routes in Western Michigan* was released in March 1993, I never expected the reaction that followed. With excerpts of the book and sample maps in hand, bike shop owners enthusiastically ordered copies of the book before it was off the presses.

The excitement that was generated by family, friends, co-workers, acquaintances and friends of co-workers was astonishing to me. I'm grateful to all who supported the first book. All of you helped fuel the drive to do a complementary book for East Michigan.

From the beginning bike club leaders from the eastern half of the state supported this project and supplied me with routes, food recommendations as well as sharing their passion for cycling and teaching me more about the nuances of cycling. A very special thanks to Ken Bawcom of the Ann Arbor Biking & Touring Society for all the time and effort he spent in seeing that his area was well represented in the book. Thanks to Joe Adams of the Tri-County Bicycle Association for supplying the maps for the three routes in the Lansing area (Grand Ledge, River Trail and Sleepy Hollow), Kathy Warszawski from the Tri-City Cyclists for her help and the maps for the Bay City, Maple Syrup and Frankenmuth routes and Gordon Sheill from the Downriver Cycling Club for the Downriver and Irish Hills routes.

For this project I'm grateful and appreciative for the support of family and friends who helped me map out and ride the routes or offered their moral support. They often had to endure endless talk about the project. Thanks to my parents, Monica, Chris, Julie, Ann, Tim, Patrick, Cindy R., Cindy G, Janet, Bob, Bonnie, Gordon, Steph, Joan, Warren, Kathy, Glennda, Paula, Dick, Gene, Sandy, Diane and Dave. Special thanks to Janet and Bob who graciously allowed me to take their picture a hundred times on Mackinac Island!

Jim DuFresne kept me inspired to stick with the project through some ups and downs. As co-authors we managed to agree through countless across-state phone calls and correspondence about the format and content. I often tapped into his bottomless reservoir of knowledge about Michigan and along the way I learned bundles from him about writing, publishing and marketing. He developed nine of the routes in this book to complete this guidebook. Thanks to Libby Richart who helped edit this book with a lively sense of humor. A special thanks to my editor, Wally Palazzolo, who knows how to clean up the kitchen without re-arranging the furniture. Much appreciation to Bob DeYoung for developing and printing black and white photographs for me and for his extra effort and enthusiasm for photography. Michele Miller once again provided excellent maps for this book and proved to be a crucial member of the "Cycling Michigan Editorial Team." Thanks for her patience and professionalism in dealing with all of us involved in the world of publishing. What a team! Thanks!

k.g.

Safety And Responsibility

Safety is an important concern in all outdoor activities. No guidebook can alert you to every hazard or anticipate the cycling ability of every reader. Therefore, the descriptions of roads and routes in this book are not representations that a particular excursion or tour will be safe for your party. When you follow any route described in this book, you assume responsibility for your own safety. Under normal conditions, such tours require the usual attention to traffic, road and trail conditions, weather, the endurance level of your party, and other factors.

Introduction

Why East Michigan?

No respect.

The east side of Michigan often gets the shaft when it comes to promotion of travel in Michigan. But East Michigan, the home for more than half of the state's residents, shouldn't be ignored. Although this region might not be as glitzy as Lake Michigan's Gold Coast or possess scenery as rugged as the Upper Peninsula, the "sunrise side" of the Lower Peninsula is scenic in its own right with an amazing variety of terrain.

What East Michigan offers for cyclists is unpretentious and uncrowded spots, urban parks, historic islands, bays, college campuses, the Lake Huron shoreline as well as river and lakeshore routes. Take a bike journey in East Michigan and you may find yourself high up on a bluff overlooking the AuSable River, enjoying the campus of Michigan State University, crossing a covered bridge, rounding the tip of the Thumb or cruising by some of the state's richest farmland.

Why East Michigan?

For this book, East Michigan is defined as the eastern half of the Lower Peninsula, from the Downriver Detroit area north to Mackinac Island, to Mount Pleasant and Lansing in the middle of the state, the Lake Huron shoreline in northeast Michigan and the Thumb region. The 30 routes in this book range from the southeast corner of the state by Flat Rock, to Cheboygan, Mackinaw City and Mackinac Island in northeast Michigan and include inland areas such as Gaylord, Lansing, Ann Arbor and Jackson.

Southeast Michigan revolves around Detroit, Michigan's largest city, but surrounding the city are the rolling hills and lakes of northern Oakland County, the bluewater region of Port Huron and the culture and college activities of Ann Arbor, home of the University of Michigan. Although none of the routes in this book are located within the Detroit city limits, many are only a short drive away, making for ideal daytrips for cycling.

Saginaw Bay to the west and Lake Huron to the east shape "the Thumb" of Michigan. Our fast-paced urban life can be easily left behind with a trip to this appendage of the Michigan mitten. The Thumb is a rural area rich in its agricultural traditions, quiet towns and uncrowded shoreline scenery. Its rural pace will soothe the most frazzled city dweller and cycling tourists will cherish its beaches, farm markets, scenic lighthouses and lightly traveled country roads.

Between 1850 and 1910, massive log drives filled the Saginaw and AuSable rivers, which were avenues to the sawmill towns on Lake Huron. Lumber baron mansions lined the streets of towns like Saginaw and Bay City. Logging devastated the Lake Huron region which led to the establishment of many forest preserves in an effort to repair and manage the land. Today, almost a century later, the forests are back in northeast Michigan. Blessed with miles of Lake Huron shoreline, inland lakes and forests, the tranquility of northeast Michigan beckons visitors. In this region of the state, an October color tour, the solitude of a shoreline campsite, panoramic vistas or cycling past towering pines form lasting memories.

The inland areas such as Lansing, our state capital, the college town of Mount Pleasant, Jackson, Ann Arbor and the Irish Hills demonstrate the diversity of East Michigan. You can cycle around

There are many bicycle clubs in East Michigan which offer group rides throughout much of the year. See the Appendix for a complete list.

a small lake in a resort area, stop at a museum along the Lansing River Trail, cross a covered bridge or amble along a rail trail. Cycling is an excellent way to find hidden corners of East Michigan and learn about our state's colorful past.

The Routes

This book describes 30 routes, ranging from 4 to more than 60 miles. It is geared for cyclists of all abilities, with an emphasis on day excursions and cycle touring. Routes can easily be lengthened or combined for a weekend or more of cycling. On all of the routes, 10 or 12-speed touring bicycles are suitable. But mountain or hybrid bicycles can be used and are even recommended on the LakeLands and Paint Creek rail trails. The routes are a mix of narrow roads with no shoulders, busy roadways with paved shoulders and bike paths through towns, woods, forests and open farm country. Most important, the tours are geared for leisurely sightseeing and eating, not competitive racing. Shorter options are ideal for beginners, families or those who simply want more time in a cafe than on the road.

The East Michigan region has been divided into four sections: Southeast, Heartland, Thumb & Tri-Cities and Northeast. Most of the routes list attractions that will be of interest to cyclists such as places to stop and eat, creative lodging ideas and bicycle shops in the area. The descriptions and directions will give you an idea of the terrain and difficulty of each ride while highlighting the unique aspects of each trip.

To develop the tours, I consulted bicycling clubs, studied state and county cycling maps and worked with local tourism officials before hitting the road and riding the routes. These are not the only places worth touring in East Michigan but they are an excellent sampling of the best East Michigan has to offer cyclists.

The shorter options have been developed with children in mind. Some of the best options for family trips include Mackinac Island, the Croswell-Lexington bike path, the Lansing River Trail, the cider mill option of the Paint Creek Trail and the bike paths in Willow Metropark and Kensington Metropark.

Climate

Be prepared because weather in Michigan changes often. Although some enthusiasts cycle year-round, May through October are the most popular months to cycle in East Michigan. Showers are frequent in April but the second half of the month often features pleasant stretches of weather in the southern half of East Michigan when the skies are blue and temperatures are a comfortable 50 to 60 degrees. Wildflowers, always a delight when cycling, will emerge along roadsides in early May and be around through much of June.

By July, temperatures can range anywhere from a pleasant 70 degrees to a blistering 90 degrees. Sunny weather and clear skies are the norm but East Michigan, like the west side of the state, is known for sudden thunderstorms that rumble across the land-scape.

If you can get away, fall is an ideal time to cycle in East Michigan. In remote spots like the Black Lake region you'll have the road to yourself in the middle of the week. From September through October temperatures return to those pleasant levels in the mid-60s. Showers are common (especially on the weekends it seems) but so are those glorious Indian summer days when the sky is azure blue, the air dry and the trees are peaking in their autumn hues of red, yellow and vivid orange. Trees begin changing colors in late September and tend to peak in early October from Gaylord to Mackinac Island, the second or third week of October in the Tri-Cities and Thumb area and late October in areas further south. Depending on the year, it's often possible to enjoy the last splashes of fall color in early November along the routes in Downriver Detroit and Hillsdale.

Cycling Trip Tip #1

If you're itching to ride in early April, then search out an asphalt bike path in Southeast Michigan. Early April can still be a soggy, wet time throughout most of the state. Dirt roads will be muddy and filled with pot holes while the shoulders along paved roads can be just as bad. But asphalt absorbs the heat of that spring sun to become a dry surface the quickest. The Metroparks of Southeast Michigan features bike paths in most of the 13 units. In 1995, the park system opened up its newest and longest path, a 12-mile, one-way route that passes through Lower Huron, Willow and Oakwoods Metroparks in Wayne Country. For more information see Tour 1 of this guide. For a map to all the parks call ☎ (800) 47-PARKS.

Riding after October? Just make sure you dress in layers and wear a winter glove system. Regardless of when you ride, always pack rain gear or at least a windbreaker, even if the sun is shining when you begin. You never know with Michigan weather!

Bicycle safety

Bicycle helmets are strongly recommended whenever you go riding. Wearing a helmet can prevent serious head injuries and reduces (some experts say by as much as 85 percent) the chances of injuring yourself if you are thrown from your bicycle. Look for the Snell or ANSI sticker on the inside of the helmet. Although helmets can be expensive, they are a necessary investment for all cyclists.

Here are some other tips for a safe trip:

Safety check your bike: Before a tour, especially a long one, perform a quick inspection of your bicycle, paying close attention to your brakes, spokes, tires and quick release hubs. Make sure everything is operating smoothly to avoid an unexpected mishap on the road.

Ride with the flow of traffic: Do not ride against the flow of traffic and do not pull off the road every time a car approaches on narrow shoulders. Be careful: the transition between roadbed and shoulder is rarely smooth and can cause you to lose control.

Increase your visibility: Wear bright colored clothes and jackets instead of darker colors or earth tones to increase your visibility with motorists.

Pay attention to the road: There is a tendency at times to daydream while cycling long distances. It's easy to do as you fall into a rhythmic trance due to the constant motion of pedaling. But be alert for road signs, intersections, and patches of loose gravel, wet leaves or unexpected pot holes.

Observe all traffic signs: More times than not cycling accidents are caused by careless cyclists. Avoid coasting through stop signs or racing through yellow lights. Treat every intersection as if you were in a car.

A cyclist pauses at the historical railroad depot in Pinckney, a favorite rest stop for riders along the LakeLands Trail State Park.

Be prepared for bothersome dogs: Some bikers carry a spray can of dog repellent that can be purchased at any good bike shop. Others simply try to "out run" the dog. Whatever, have a plan ready for when a snapping mutt is chasing you.

Packing For A Bike Tour

Always bring plenty of water. If there is any room in your bike bags after you've packed the other necessities (fruit chewies, boxes of fruit juice, a pound of trail mix, etc.) you might want to throw in a few tools. The four most common breakdowns for cyclists on the roads are flat tires, a broken brake cable, a suddenly wobbling wheel and an off-sprocket chain.

All four can be repaired at roadside if you have the right tools. Here's a list of suggested tools. Pack what the distance and number of days you'll be on the road dictate:

Crescent wrench: Don't ride anywhere without one. It's useful to change a tire, adjust spokes and tighten any nut or bolt that comes loose.

Tire irons: Three plastic ones are lightweight and make changing a tire a lot easier.

Tube patch kit: Along with the kit, you should pack along a spare tube on long rides or routes that include dirt roads.

Frame-mounted tire pump: How else are you going to inflate the spare or add some extra air to your tires?

Screwdrivers: Both a slot and a Phillips head type. Your best bet is to invest in a small tool kit from a bike shop designed to provide what you need when repairing your bike on the road or be easily stored in a compact case when you're not.

Small can of WD-40: It's nice to carry some lubrication along on those multi-day bike tours.

This and that: Depending on your bike model, you might want Allen wrenches, vise grip pliers and a little duct tape and paper clips when all else fails. It's amazing what you can repair with a piece of tape and a paper clip.

One more thing; either know how to make the necessary repairs, pack along the manual or ride with a friend who can. All the tools in the world are useless if you don't know what you're doing.

Karen's Favorites

Every route in this book is special in its own way. To have some fun, I came up with these categories to serve as a further guide.

Most historical: Island Tour.

Most wooded and remote: Black Lake Tour.

Best for kids: This is a toss-up between Mackinac Island with its cannons and muskets or the Lansing River Trail with its museums, zoo and Planet Walk.

Best for large groups: Sharon Mills Winery Tour.

Best workout for experienced cyclists: Natural Gaylord.

Fastest, flattest route: Showboat Tour (Chesaning) or Little Bavaria Tour (Frankenmuth).

Most scenic: Irish Hills.

Most fudge per mile: Mackinac Island.

Best lakeshore route: Tip O' The Thumb Tour (Port Austin).

Best ice cream stop: Cook's Dairy Farm on the The Lakes Loop (Oakland County).

And finally the most beer, bowling and bait per mile: toss-up between Bay City Area Tour and Harsens Island.

Happy Cycling!!!

Cycling Trip Tip #2

Bicycle helmets absorb the impact of a blow to the head through the padding and foam of their liners. If you experience a particularly hard fall from a bicycle the liner could become crushed and then offer far less protection the next time you take a spill. Even though the destruction might not be obvious, you should consider replacing a helmet after such a serious blow.

Most Southeast Michigan routes wind pass inland lakes, rivers or Lake St. Clair.

 Southeast Michigan

Downriver Ramble
Island Pedal
Huron River Ride
Winery Tour
Kensington Tour
Paint Creek Trail
The Lakes Loop
Harsens Island

Many of the Huron-Clinton Metroparks, including Oakwoods, feature paved bike paths.

1

Downriver Ramble

Trip Card

Starting Point: Rockwood
Counties: Monroe, Wayne
Distance: 40 miles
Shorter option: 10 miles round trip
Terrain: Flat
Highlights: Huron River, three Metroparks, cider mills
Suggested riders: beginners to intermediate

Downriver? Down river from what?

When someone in Southeast Michigan says "Downriver," they're not talking about which way the water is flowing but a destination, an unique area of blue collar communities intermingled with farms, orchards and a few steel mills, linked together by the Huron River and located just down the Detroit River from that urban sprawl known as metropolitan Detroit.

This route in Monroe County and southern Wayne County, featuring flat roads, light traffic and many parks, is a great respite for those in the more congested areas up river. Gordon Sheill, touring chairperson for the Downriver Cycling Club (the "Best in the Midwest" as they call it) supplied the basis for this route. It's a ride with variety; a road that closely parallels the Huron River, the small town of Flat Rock, the pleasant burg of Waltz and three units of the Huron-Clinton Metroparks; Lake Erie, Willow and Oakwoods.

The Metroparks, a 13-unit system in five counties, protects 23,000 acres of the watershed of the Huron and Clinton rivers. Both Willow and Oakwoods are connected by the Huron River and a paved bike path that makes for an ideal 10-mile family ride with an interesting nature center at the halfway point.

The Downriver Cycling Club often uses a modified version of the 40-mile loop as one of their evening rides where club members can forget their worries for a while and discuss whether to stop at Kate's Kitchen in Flat Rock or the Carleton House restaurant in Carleton.

To reach Lake Erie Metropark, depart I-75 at exit 26 and head east on Huron River Drive, following the signs to Jefferson Road (keep in mind that Huron River Drive is on the north side of the river and South Huron Road parallels the south side). The park entrance is just left (north) on Jefferson. There is a small motor vehicle fee to enter any metropark, except on Tuesday when admission is free. Lake Erie Metropark is a great place to begin and end a ride but if you just have to save $3, you can park at the Foodtown Mini Mall at the corner of Huron River Drive and Fort Street in Rockwood at Mile 2.3 of the ride.

This Downriver cycling route can easily be combined with the 20-mile Grosse Ile route (see Tour 2) for a pleasant weekend of cycling. For a description of the bike paths in another unit of the Huron-Clinton Metroparks, see Kensington Metropark (Tour 5).

Stage one (11 miles) Lake Erie Metropark overlooks the spot where the Detroit River flows into the Great Lake. The park includes picnic areas along Lake Erie, shelters, bathrooms and a food concession. There is even a wave pool here, a golf course (how about 18 holes of golf after a 40 mile ride?) and a new Waterfowler's Museum that opened in 1995.

From the park entrance turn left (south) on Jefferson Road and within a quarter mile right (west) on Huron River Drive. This is practically the only road you follow in the first leg and for the most part it's newly resurfaced with paved shoulders. You begin

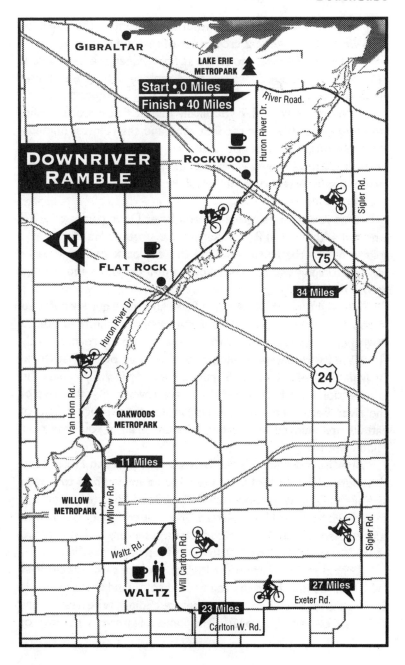

by passing a few fields but within a mile enter the town of Rockwood and at **Mile 2** cross a set of railroad tracks.

In a third of a mile, you arrive at Fort Street, the commercial heart of Rockwood. Cross this road with care and be watchful along this stretch as it passes an exit off I-75. At times the traffic can be heavy. At **Mile 2.7** you finally depart Rockwood's traffic, see the Huron River for the first time and then almost immediately reach the fringes of Flat Rock, a larger community. The heart of this Downriver town is reached at **Mile 5.3**, when you come to the busy intersection at Telegraph Road. Just to the south here is a Dairy Queen.

After you cross Telegraph, Huron River Drive comes to a "T" junction with Arsenal Road. Across the street is Hu Rock Park, split in half by the Huron River. In this city park you'll find bathrooms, drinking water, picnic tables and a delightful foot bridge across the river.

Turn right (north) on Arsenal Road and you'll quickly come to a stop sign where Huron River Drive resumes (the road does a dogleg curve on Telegraph). Turn left (west) and the road, recently resurfaced with paved shoulders, will take you out of Flat Rock. At **Mile 6** there is a major "S" curve and at **Mile 7.5** you pass the intersection with Inkster Road and are rewarded with views of the river. Better views of the Huron flowing through a field of cattails are enjoyed in another mile and half as you pass near Middlebelt Road.

At **Mile 9.5** Huron River Drive curves past Van Horn Road and Huron High School and in less than a mile comes to a stop sign at the "T" intersection with Willow Road. For the first time in the trip you depart Huron River Drive as it continues north. You turn left (south) on Willow Road, pass a cemetery and then arrive at the posted entrance to Oakwoods Metropark at **Mile 11**.

Right at the entrance is the Metropark bike path that extends in both directions from the road. Head south and the path winds 3 miles through fields and woods before ending at the nature center in Oakwoods Metropark. The center features a number of hands-on natural exhibits, including a great indoor turtle pond, as well as several foot trails and a scenic overview of the Huron River. Time it right and you might be able to enjoy a ride in its Voyageurs' canoe. The center ☎ (313-782-3956) is open 10 a.m. to 5 p.m. daily except weekdays during the school year when its hours are 1-5 p.m. (mornings are reserved for school groups).

Head north and the bike path takes you into Willow Metropark past several picnic areas, including the Big Bend area where you can sit at a picnic table on the banks of the Huron River. This 40-mile tour doesn't include mileage for trips into either park. Add 6 miles to visit the nature center, 4 miles to follow the loop through Willow Metropark. Both parks have bathrooms, shelters and drinking water.

Stage two (14 miles) From the entrance to Oakwoods Metropark, continue west on Willow Road and at **Mile 12.6** you pass the south entrance into Willow Metropark (there is also an entrance on its west side). You reach the bypass over I-275 in less than a half mile, perhaps the steepest slope you have to climb on this route, cross a set of railroad tracks in less than a mile and then enter the hamlet of Willow at **Mile 14**. There is a small store here but if you need to stop for something to drink or eat, *wait!*

Willow Road continues west and in a third of a mile comes to stop sign at Waltz Road. At this intersection there are signs for two cider mills. Davis Orchards is the closest and is reached by heading 1.3 miles west on Willow Road. But a much more delightful place to stop is Apple Charlie's on South Huron Road. Turn right (north) on Waltz Road and in 1.5 miles turn right (west) on South Huron Road to reach the cider mill in a half mile.

Apple Charlie's features an apple press and mill where you can watch the fruit being crushed during the cider season. There's also an ice cream counter, farmer's market and a bakery that sells homemade doughnuts, giant pumpkin-shaped cookies and apple-cinnamon bread. *Warning: the apple-cinnamon bread is so good there is a tendency to eat the whole loaf before leaving the cider mill, causing a severe stomach ache five miles into the ride.* There are also bathrooms here, picnic tables outside and a small eating area inside. From late June through November the mill is open daily from 8 a.m. until dusk.

Backtrack 2 miles to the intersection with Willow Road and continue south on Waltz Road. This road has a smooth surface, paved shoulders and usually light traffic. At **Mile 19.3,** you enter the hamlet of Waltz, a delightful little Downriver community. The center of town is the Waltz Inn, established in 1900 and still serving food and drinks, while nearby, overlooking the tracks, is the bright red Waltz Feed Store.

After you cycle through the town, Waltz Road makes a big curve at **Mile 20** and within a quarter mile comes to a stop sign at Oakville-Waltz Road. To the left is I-275 with bike paths. This stretch of path along I-275 is closed south of this point due to its bridges being out. Turn right (west) on Oakville-Waltz Road where at **Mile 22** you curve south onto Clark Road briefly before continuing west. At **Mile 23**, turn left (south) on West Carleton Road. The road is extremely bumpy at first with no shoulders but quickly improves. Within a mile the road curves to the east and then at **Mile 25** curves back to the south only to face another curve to the east as West Carleton Road heads into the town of Carleton. Those who need supplies or beverages can follow the road 2 miles into Carleton and then return to the tour by heading south on Grafton Road to Sigler Road. This tour, however, passes up West Carleton Road curve by continuing south on Exeter Road.

Stage three (15 miles) Exeter Road has light traffic and is a scenic ride past corn fields and barns. Within a mile you past Scofield Carleton Road heading east and at **Mile 27** you turn left (east) on Sigler Road. You will stay on this road for the next 10 miles.

Sigler Road, with narrow gravel shoulders and light traffic, is an avenue through the country for the most part. You cross a set of railroad tracks within a half mile and then at **Mile 29** arrive at

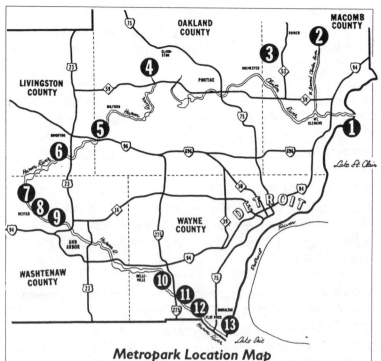

Metropark Location Map

The 13-unit Metropark system covers 23,000 acres in the Huron and Clinton rivers watershed. Almost every park features paved bike trails that are ideal for family rides.

1. Metro Beach
2. Wolcott Mill
3. Stony Creek
4. Indian Springs
5. Kensington
6. Huron Meadows
7. Hudson Mills
8. Dexter-Huron
9. Delhi
10. Lower Huron
11. Willow
12. Oakwoods
13. Lake Erie

a stop sign on Grafton Road. You continue east and in the next 2 miles cross a bypass over I-275 and then come to Telegraph Road, a very busy four-lane road, at *Mile 31.5*.

On the other side Sigler still maintains it rural appearance but an increasing number of houses have popped up along with a motorhome park. At *Mile 34* you pedal over I-75 and then several sets of tracks in the next mile before reaching Dixie Highway, another busy intersection that must be carefully crossed.

The ride along Sigler finally ends at **Mile 37.5** when you reach U.S. Turnpike. Turn left (north) and you will immediately cross the Huron River. Just on the north side of the bridge is Riverfront Park. This scenic park is managed by Brownstone Township and for the most part is for people launching their boats. But it also has restrooms and a walkway with benches that overlook the mouth of the Huron River and the marshes that border the Lake Erie shoreline.

At the park, U.S. Turnpike becomes Jefferson Road and the final 2 miles of the tour is a ride north along this road that features paved shoulders. Within a half mile of reaching Lake Erie Metropark, you pass the flashing light at the intersection at Huron River Drive.

Shorter Option (10 miles) The bike paths in Oakwoods and Willow metroparks can be combined for a 10-mile ride that most children, even those as young as seven years, can handle. Begin in Willow Metropark at the pool parking area. Located here is the Tot Lot, a playground of small houses, stores and a train where toddlers to five year-olds can play in the "Village of Willow." There are even paved streets and stop signs in this miniature town.

You can pick up the bike path near the parking lot and by following it in a clockwise direction will cycle past the Huron River before departing the park. After crossing Willow Road you immediately enter Oakwoods Metropark where the path extends 3 miles south and ends at the nature center.

Bicycle sales, service

Buffalo Bob Bicycle Repair, 26330 E. Huron River Dr., Flat Rock; ☎ (313) 782-1790.

Don's Bicycle Sales & Service, 26260 Gibraltar, Flat Rock; ☎ (313) 782-1200.

Al Petri & Sons Bicycle Centers, 2160 Fort St., Lincoln Park; ☎ (313) 381-2832.

Bicycle Bob's, 44 S. Monroe, Monroe; ☎ (313) 241-5340.

Jack's Bicycle & Fitness, 225 N. Telegraph, Monroe; ☎ (313) 242-1400.

Sensational Beginnings, 300 Detroit Ave., Monroe; ☎ (313) 242-9613.

Easy Rider Bike Shop, 23007 Eureka, Taylor; ☎ (313) 374-7433.

Al Petri & Sons Bicycle Center, 22720 Allen Road, Woodhaven; ☎ (313) 675-5567.

Tarjeft & Sons Bicycle, 5719 Wilson, Trenton; ☎ (313) 676-3541.

Area attractions

Monroe County Historical Museum, Navarre-Anderson Trading Post, River Raisin Battlefield Visitor Center, ☎ (313) 243-7137.

Waterfowler's Museum, Lake Erie Metropark, ☎ (313) 379-5020.

Area events & festivals

May: Flat Rock Antiques & Flea Market, Flat Rock; Waltz Homecoming, Waltz.

June: Rockwood St. Mary's Festival, Rockwood; Monroe Arts & Crafts Show.

July: Gibraltar Independence Day Festival; Knights of Columbus Festival, Monroe; Carleton Rotary Community Festival, Carleton.

August: Monroe County Fair, Monroe County Fairgrounds (3 miles west of Monroe), Old French Town Days, Monroe.

September: Flat Rock Riverfest, Flat Rock.

October: Flat Rock Antiques & Flea Market.

Travel information

Monroe County Tourism Bureau; ☎ (800) 252-3011.

Huron-Clinton Metroparks; ☎ (800) 47-PARKS.

The Grosse Ile bike tour features many historical markers and 19th century homes along the Detroit River.

2

Island Pedal

Trip Card

Starting point: Trenton
County: Wayne
Distance: 20 miles
Shorter option: 8 miles
Terrain: Flat
Highlights: the Detroit River, historical sites and homes
Suggested Riders: Beginners to intermediate

There are dozens of islands in the Detroit River but only one is known as "The Island." Grosse Ile is the largest, the most historical and, from a cyclist's point of view, the only one that can provide a scenic half-day ride.

The south end of Grosse Ile overlooks Lake Erie while its north end is across from the Downriver city of Wyandotte. In between is an island that is eight miles long, 1.5 miles at its widest point and sits in the middle of the Detroit River with Canada on one side and the U.S. on the other.

Grosse Ile is steeped in history. It's said that French explorers, including Sieur de La Salle, landed on the Island before they founded the settlement of Detroit in 1701. On July 6, 1776, William Macomb purchased Grosse Ile from four Indian tribes and there have been residents and history on the Island ever since. That's obvious to cyclists as they will pass a half dozen or so green markers designating a Michigan Historical Site.

But this ride is also scenic as well as historical. The vast majority of the ride is along the Detroit River where boat traffic ranges from walleye fishermen and water skiers to huge ore-carrying freighters and international ships bound for the other side of the Atlantic. Many of the homes on the east side of the Island are historical mansions built in the 19th century.

The only drawback to pedalling the Island is the lack of a paved shoulder on East River and West River roads, which make up the majority of this 20-mile route. These roads wind so close to the edge of the bluffs above the Detroit River there's simply no room for much of a shoulder, paved or otherwise. While Grosse Ile Township has built a bike path and is planning to extend it in the future, the network is in the center of the Island and away from the scenic stretches along the river.

The saving grace of the Island is the lack of a commercial area. Most stores and businesses are located on Macomb Street in the middle of the Island and the areas you will be riding are strictly residential. Still, this is not a good route to undertake on a Friday afternoon when there will be scores of "Islanders" scurrying home after a long week at the office.

This loop conveniently begins and ends at Atwood Park in Trenton across the river from Grosse Ile. From I-75, depart at exit 32 and head east on West Road into Trenton. In 3 miles, turn north (left) from West Road onto West Jefferson and in a few blocks turn east (right) on Atwood Street which dead ends at the park overlooking the Detroit River.

Stage One (9 miles) At Atwood Park, you'll find bathrooms, parking, picnic tables, grills for a possible post-ride feast and a riverwalk with a panoramic view of where you'll be riding later. Head up the hill and then turn left on Riverside Road, a quiet residential street with sidewalks on both sides.

Within 0.7 mile, you'll turn right on Walnut Road and immediately pass an A&W Root Beer outlet. This historical A&W, which is drive-in only, has been serving up frosty mugs of root beer for

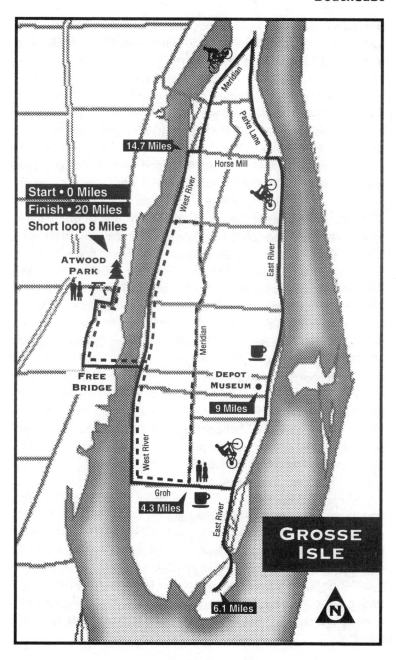

Meridian

Parke Lane

14.7 Miles

Horse Mill

Start • 0 Miles

Finish • 20 Miles

Short loop 8 Miles

West River

East River

ATWOOD
PARK

Meridian

DEPOT
MUSEUM

9 Miles

FREE
BRIDGE

West River

Groh

4.3 Miles

East River

6.1 Miles

GROSSE
ISLE

N

almost half a century and is a tough place for cyclists to pass up on the way back. From Walnut you turn left onto Elizabeth Road to avoid busy West Jefferson Road entirely.

Elizabeth Road will lead over the bridge into Elizabeth Park which is operated by Wayne County. The park road is a one-way loop, past picnic tables, swings and an impressive pavilion along the Detroit River. At the very back of it, 1.5 miles from the start, is a gate to enter the Elizabeth Park Marina. Cut through the marina parking lot to reach Parkway Road and the Free Bridge across the river to the Island. If this gate is locked, don't despair. There is a path along the fence that will quickly lead to Parkway.

Grosse Ile has two bridges. At the north end of the Island is the privately owned Toll Bridge. The Free Bridge is maintained by Wayne Country and has sidewalks on each side of it. Be careful of Parkway, it's a busy road, but it's only 50 yards or less from the marina entrance until you're on the bridge. From the middle of the bridge, you'll have a scenic view of the river and on a clear day even the tip of Lake Erie.

Cross the Free Bridge and on east side immediately swing left off Parkway onto a road posted as West River Road. This road descends gently to a stop sign and junction with the true West River Road. Turn left (south) here to immediately pass the marina for Water's Edge Golf Course. At **Mile 2.4** you'll pass Bellevue Road. At the corner of Bellevue and West River Road is the golf course clubhouse open to the public for meals and refreshments.

Continue south on West River Road, a street with narrow gravel shoulders. The views of the river, however, are excellent. After cycling past the Detroit Edison Power Plant on the Trenton side, the scenery will improve immensely.

At **Mile 3.5** West River Road makes a sharp 90-degree curve and becomes Groh Street. Groh will lead across the Island to East River Road by cutting through the Grosse Ile Airport. During World War II and for 25 years after that, the airport was a major Naval Air Station, complete with dozens of barracks, huge hangers and an Olympic-size swimming pool for the servicemen. At **Mile 4.3** you arrive at the junction with Meridian Road and one end of the Island's bike path. Near here are the Pilot House with a phone and restrooms and the Airport Inn, a small bar with hamburgers on its menu.

Continue east on Groh to reach East River road at **Mile 4.8**. First head south (right) on East River and follow the road 1.5 miles as it takes you on a scenic stretch to Hickory Island. You'll pedal across a short causeway where there are views of the river on both sides and then end at Hickory Island Yacht Club and its impressive armada of sailboats. At this point backtrack to the corner of Groh and East River, reached at **Mile 7.6 miles**.

Continue north on East River, a road with wide paved shoulders along this stretch. At **Mile 8.3**, you come to a stop sign at the corner of East River and Manchester Road. At this point East River makes an S-turn to return to the edge of the river bluffs which means you return to great views but lose the wide shoulders. Quickly you come to the first Michigan historical marker about the stockade that the U.S. Army built and maintained on the Island shortly after the War of 1812.

At **Mile 9**, you arrive at the old Michigan Central Railroad Depot on the corner of East River and Parkway. Built in 1904, the depot has since been renovated into a museum by the Grosse Ile Historical Society. Behind it is the U.S. Customs House, and both buildings have displays and exhibits that cover the intriguing history of the Island. Hours are 10 a.m. to noon Thursday and 1-4 p.m. Sunday. Admission is by donations. The museum's front lawn makes for a great place to take a snack or juice break while watching the river traffic.

Stage Two (11 miles) From the depot museum continue north on East River Road, where you will pass a string of 19th century mansions all within a district listed on the National Register of Historical Places. Within a quarter mile you'll come to the corner of East River and Macomb, where you'll pass an observation deck that overlooks the river. Just 50 yards down Macomb is

Nates Market for refreshments.

Continue north on East River where you quickly pass a stone monument that marks the location of the Treaty Tree, the place where William Macomb and his brother Alexander purchased the Island from the Potawatomi Indians. Just beyond is Grosse Ile Middle School, including its historical 1910 building.

East River still has little shoulder along this stretch so use caution if you're riding during a busy period of the day. At **Mile 10.6**, you reach St. Anne Chapel at the corner of Church Road and East River. The stone chapel is a photographer's delight while there's a small parking area along the river that makes for a good place to take a break.

Continuing north on East River, at **Mile 11.2** you reach the historical marker dedicated to Mexican and Civil War hero Col. Thorton Fleming, whose stone library can still be seen off the road. In another third of a mile East River ends when you take a 90-degree turn to merge into Horse Mill Road, whose name is explained by yet another Michigan historic marker just up the road.

Just before the green marker, however, turn north (right) on Parke Lane. Within a half mile you cross a stone bridge over the Canal. Grosse Ile is technically several islands and it is divided in the middle by this long narrow canal. Follow Parke Lane past more impressive riverfront homes and then at **Mile 13.3** you make a 180-degree turn onto Meridian Road. This stretch of Meridian is hard packed dirt in a heavily forested area. The dirt portion lasts almost a mile but most road bikes will have few problems handling the surface. If you want to avoid it, keep heading down Horse Mill Road to West Road, bypassing Parke Lane and Meridian all together.

The dirt portion of Meridian ends at the corner of Bridge Road where you can look west and see the Toll Bridge. Continue south on Meridian which briefly becomes the Island's "only divided highway," with wide paved shoulders. At **Mile 14.7** turn west (right) onto Horse Mill Road which will quickly swing south

The 1904 Michigan Central Railroad Depot is today a museum.

(left) into West River Road.

You begin the final leg of the journey by looking at mammoth McLouth Steel Mill, but once past the sinister-looking plant, the view from West River returns to placid river scenes. At **Mile 16.6** you pass West Shore Golf and Country Club, one of three on the Island, and at **Mile 17.5** you recross the Canal. Here you pedal underneath the approach to the Free Bridge and then immediately turn left to reach Parkway Road.

Recross the bridge and return to Atwood along the same route used to cut through Elizabeth Park at the beginning. Hungry? There's not only the A&W on the way back but if you remain on West Jefferson you will enter what is commonly referred to as "Old Trenton", where there are several restaurants. Elloit's Bakery is the place to go for a cup of coffee and a gooey donut to re-energize yourself after the 20-mile pedal.

Shorter Option (8 miles) This optional loop begins and ends on Grosse Ile and utilizes the Island's bike path that runs along Meridian Road. There are plans to extend the bike path but presently it's a 3-mile route that begins at Church Road and ends at the Grosse Ile Airport at Groh Road. You can park at the old Youth Center and follow Meridian Road 0.4 mile to pick up the north end of the bike path. At Groh Road head west (right) to reach West River Road and follow it back to Church Road, a ride of 3 miles. Turn east (right) Church to reach Meridian and backtrack to the parking lot.

Bicycle sales, service

Al Petri & Sons Bicycle Centers, 22720 Allen, Woodhaven, 48183; ☎ (313) 675-8655.

Tarjeft & Sons Bicycle Shop, 5719 Wilson, Trenton, 48183; ☎(313) 676-3541.

Easy Rider Bike Shop, 23007 Eureka, Taylor, 48180; ☎ (313) 374-7433.

Area Attractions

Grosse Ile Historical Museum, Parkway and East River Rd., ☎ (313) 675-2550.

Travel information

Grosse Ile Township Office, 8841 Macomb; ☎ (313) 676-4422.

Cycling Trip Tip #3

Try putting your tire repair kit and whatever tools needed on a long trip in an old tube sock before placing them in your saddle bag or fanny pack. This keeps them organized and prevents excessive rattling. Then if you need to make a repair, you can wear the sock on your hand to avoid greasy fingers.

⟨3⟩

Huron River Ride

Trip Card

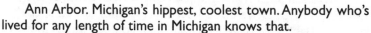

Starting point: Ann Arbor
Counties: Washtenaw, Livingston
Distance: 60 miles
Shorter option: 4 to 12 miles
Terrain: flat to rolling hills
Highlights: Ann Arbor, Huron River, Pinckney
Recreation Area, Brighton Recreation Area
Suggested riders: intermediate to advanced

Ann Arbor. Michigan's hippest, coolest town. Anybody who's lived for any length of time in Michigan knows that.

Ken Bawcom, one of the leaders of the Ann Arbor Bicycle Touring Society (AABTS) and a long-time resident of the city, says he likes Ann Arbor because it's not like the real world. It's a place where you can be an eternal student, a place with delicatessens to rival those in the East, jazz radio stations and festivals, blues concerts, Big Ten football and one of the largest art extravaganzas in the country - the Ann Arbor Art Fair, which takes place each year in July.

As a college town and a hip place to live and work, it naturally figures that Ann Arbor is a bike-friendly region. Lots of bike shops, bike rentals, bike paths and bike lanes dot the town. You can even rent a bicycle for a month from the Student Bike Shop in Ann Arbor.

This 60-mile route, developed by AABTS, is a fine example of the range of terrain, scenery and food stops the area has to offer. Combine a visit to Ann Arbor with a tour of the surrounding countryside. Cycle by the Huron River, through two popular recreation areas and take the road to Hell (Hell, Michigan that is, and not a bad place at that!).

Stage one (10.2 miles) Wheeler Park is located north of the downtown Ann Arbor area. It is surrounded by North Fourth and Fifth avenues, and Beakes and Summit streets. There is off-road parking on streets near the park, which is a popular starting point for the AABTS. Cycle left (west) onto Depot, a busy four-lane road, and then take a right (north) onto North Main Street, another busy four-lane road heading north out of town. Very quickly you'll make a sharp left (west) to get to Huron River Drive, a somewhat tricky corner. Be especially careful of approaching traffic to your right as you make your way across the street to get to Huron River Drive.

As Huron River Drive is a winding, twisting road along the river, it's not the fastest thoroughfare to anywhere. It can be busy, although motorists are tolerant and used to sharing the road with bicyclists.

The tree-lined section of the road is exceptionally pretty, with wildflowers in season and glimpses of the river. Some of the hills on Huron River Drive can be deceiving as they are steeper than they look with a lot of gradual uphills. Of course, you're rewarded with some long downhills.

At **Mile 2** on your right is Barton Park, another alternative starting point. Following that is a little bit of open country, a gradual uphill cresting at **Mile 3.1**, and rolling hills. Within a half mile you can almost reach out and touch the river after passing Maple Road and a small parking area to your right. The road makes a sharp curve to your right before you pass Wagner Road and cross over railroad tracks, followed by a long curve downhill and a gradual uphill cresting at **Mile 5.3**. In July, you just might see periwinkle wildflowers dotting this section of the road.

The 50-acre Delhi Metropark is on your left at **Mile 6**. This park has picnic facilities, canoeing, fishing and hiking trails, plus cross country skiing in the winter! Next there's an odd intersection with a bridge and the Huron River to your left. Caution: Watch for cars exiting private drives at this point. Huron River Drive starts to wind, dip and roll with the hills and curves. You

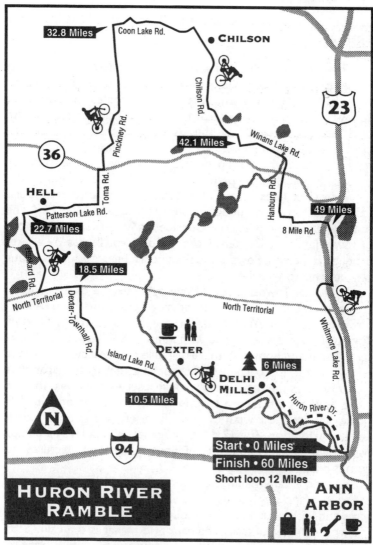

32.8 Miles

Coon Lake Rd.

CHILSON

Chilson Rd.

23

Pinckney Rd.

Winans Lake Rd.

36

42.1 Miles

Toma Rd.

Hanburg Rd.

HELL

Patterson Lake Rd.

49 Miles

22.7 Miles

8 Mile Rd.

18.5 Miles

Unadilla Rd.

Dexter-Townhall Rd.

North Territorial

North Territorial

Whitmore Lake Rd.

DEXTER

6 Miles

Island Lake Rd.

DELHI MILLS

Huron River Dr.

10.5 Miles

N

94

Start • 0 Miles
Finish • 60 Miles
Short loop 12 Miles

HURON RIVER RAMBLE

ANN ARBOR

pass through an exceptional tunnel of trees and then at *Mile 9* Dexter-Huron Metropark appears on your left. The park is open from 8 a.m. to 9 p.m.

There's a long, gradual uphill curving to your right through yet another tunnel of trees at *Mile 9.5*. If you're in need of liquids or energy boosters, stop at the Dexter Party Store at the intersection of Huron River Drive and Mast Road reached in a little over a half mile.

Stage two (16.2 miles) Cycle left (south) onto Mast Road into the village limits of Dexter. The Dexter Mill will be on your right at **Mile 10.5** while Mast Road becomes Central Street in town. Cruise into downtown Dexter, which has stores with brick facades, an A&W and the AATBS favorite, the Dexter Bakery. Do what club members do - try out the bakery's muffins and rolls and rest at the small park just west of the bakery. There are even vault toilets at the park that the AATBS helped fund.

Turn right (west) onto Main Street, which turns into Island Lake Road. You'll cycle under a one-lane bridge at **Mile 11.4**. The road has gravel shoulders on both sides as you make your way out of town. Just past Dexter-Pinckney Road, you'll pass by a farm produce stand with flowers and sweet corn before you make your way up a hill to your left.

In Dexter Township you'll cycle by a mixture of trees, fields, residential sections and a classic red barn before you reach Dexter-Townhall Road at **Mile 14.4**. Turn right (north) onto Dexter-Townhall Road, a scenic road with a mix of wildflowers and scattered barns and homes. Within a half mile the road curves to your left; watch for approaching traffic from a street to the right. Pass Colby Road as the road winds through a series of curves. You can judge how good the corn crop is by the cornfields on your left (knee-high by the Fourth of July!). Turn left (west) onto North Territorial Road at **Mile 17.4**. North Territorial Road is a bit bumpy with gravel shoulders but the wildflowers, barns and picturesque homes make the ride worthwhile.

There's a campground to your right at **Mile 18.5** which is part of the Pinckney Recreation Area. The state park unit is 10,842 acres and without a doubt the mountain biking hot spot in Michigan with 40 miles of trails. The park also manages the LakeLands Rail-Trail (see Tour 9). Cyclists with mountain bikes may want to combine the road route described in this chapter with the trails in the Pinckney Recreation Area. The most popular trails are Crooked Lake Loop (5 miles), and Potawatomi Trail (17 miles).

Urban dwellers will find solace in the Pinckney Recreation Area with its lakes, ponds, marshes, ridges and hills. Forested primarily in hardwoods, the area lights up with wildflowers, dazzles visitors with its fall colors and is a haven for a diversity of wildlife including deer, fox, pheasants and a large number of waterfowl.

In the Pinckney Recreation Area, turn right (north) onto Hankerd Road at *Mile 19*, a lightly traveled, two-lane road that makes a few dips. As you cycle past North Lake Road, you'll encounter some rolling hills through a heavily wooded section. There's a hiking trail crossing at *Mile 21.3* followed by more hills and the Highland Lake access point within a mile. Turn right (east) onto Patterson Lake Road at *Mile 22.7*. This two-lane road, with primarily gravel shoulders, is not heavily traveled. The road twists and turns as you make your way to Hell.

Actually, the small hamlet of Hell is not such a bad place. There are nice homes, and well-kept barns. The Hell Creek Party Store at *Mile 23.7* is the place for souvenirs and refreshments. You will cycle by another red barn along Patterson Lake Road and then pass Cedar Lake Road as you make your way back to Ann Arbor.

Cycle left at the arrow pointing toward Patterson Lake at *Mile 25.9*. The road changes to Pinckney Road, which is still a paved two-lane road with gravel shoulders, before you reach the Pinckney Village limits at *Mile 26.4*. As you make your way into town the road is called South Howell. On the main street in town there are several options for eating, including another AATBS favorite, the Pinckney Inn, famous for their Belgian waffles and western omelettes.

Pinckney is a scenic town with gift shops and the conveniently located Village Cyclery, if you're in need of quick repairs or feel like a new pair of bike gloves. Across from Village Cyclery in downtown Pinckney is a small park, an excellent place to take a break. The park has a gazebo, restrooms, and a picnic area to rest those weary legs!

Stage three (17.6 miles) Head east on M-36 to depart town. Cycle left at the sign pointing to Howell. This narrow, two-lane road is called Pearl in town, then D-19 and eventually Pinckney Road. Very shortly you'll be in open country. There are some nice hills on this road that either has no shoulders or narrow gravel ones. There's a long downhill followed by an uphill at *Mile 29.8* and then within a half mile the road levels out. Within 3 miles,

Huron River Drive is one of most popular and scenic routes for cyclists starting out in Ann Arbor. (Photo by Ken Bawcom)

you'll turn right (east) onto Coon Lake Road, which will take you toward the Brighton Recreation Area.

This road is a bit bumpy as it twists and curves with views of Crooked Lake to your left. The "Welcome to Genoa Township" sign is at **Mile 34**. Turn right (south) on Chilson Road, a lightly traveled road with gravel shoulders on either side of the road. You'll cycle by some upscale homes before passing Brighton Road at **Mile 38** closely followed by the Bishop Lake Campground in a half mile. On your right will be Brighton Recreation Area head-quarters. This 5,000-acre unit of the state park system is blessed with 10 lakes and a five-mile trail through a hardwood forest of maple, hickory and oak. The east side of Chilson Road is the site of the park's four campgrounds, frontier cabins and trail system. This is a great place to go hiking after your ride!

Turn left (east) onto Swarthout at **Mile 39.8**, a somewhat bumpy, two-lane road with many curves and hills. Before you turn left (east) onto Winans Lake Road at **Mile 42**, you'll cycle by a golf course and no doubt enjoy the wildflowers near Winans Lake that the road skirts. You'll cycle by homes with large, sloping yards before the road becomes Hamburg Road at **Mile 43.8**.

You'll notice more traffic on the road as you cross over a river at **Mile 44**. Turn left onto M-36 as you make your way to Ham-burg. There are plenty of eateries here, including a carry-out pizza place and Sheila's Country Kitchen.

Stage four (16 miles) Turn right onto Hamburg Road at **Mile 44.7** and follow the road as it curves sharply to the south and takes you out of Hamburg. You'll cycle down a steep hill past a historic cemetery at **Mile 45**. To make your way to Eight Mile Road, turn left (east) onto Sheldon Road, which jogs to the right and becomes Hall Road before turning left (east) onto Eight Mile Road. You'll cross over the freeway (M-23) via the overpass before making a right (south) onto Whitmore Lake Road. At this point, Ann Arbor's Wheeler Park is still 11 miles away. Whitmore Lake Road parallels busy US-23 and eventually crosses back over to the west side of it. Whitmore Lake Road is a lightly travelled road which makes you glad you're on a bike when watching that high-way traffic at rush hour!

After entering town (Whitmore Lake Road deadends at a small

park), veer to the left at a slight angle onto Barton Shore Drive which will turn into Barton Drive. Cycle a half mile on Barton before turning right (east) onto Pontiac Trail, a residential road. Turn right (south) onto Broadway where you'll cross the Huron River and then make a right (west) onto Summit Street and pedal back to Wheeler Park.

Time for fun! There's usually something happening in Ann Arbor. The highly-rated Zingerman's, a New York-style deli with gourmet food and a huge selection of deli sandwiches, is located near the park. Other eateries and distinctive shops are part of the Kerrytown Shops on North Fifth Avenue. Enjoy a Farmers' Market here every Wednesday and Saturday and an Artisan's Market on Sunday.

Shorter option (4 to 12 miles) Cycle from Wheeler Park to Huron River Drive as far as you want to go and backtrack to the park. There are several nice places to stop along the river, such as Barton Park at *Mile 2* or Delhi Metropark at *Mile 6* on Huron River Drive.

Bicycle service, sales

Cycle Cellar, 220 Felch, Ann Arbor; ☎ (313) 769-1115.

Student Bike Shop, 607 S. Forest, Ann Arbor; ☎ (313) 662-6986.

Ann Arbor Cyclery, 1224 Packard, Ann Arbor; ☎ (313) 761-2749.

Campus Bike & Toy Center, 514 E. William, Ann Arbor; ☎ (313) 662-0035.

Great Lakes Fitness & Cycling, 560 S. Main St., Ann Arbor; ☎ (313) 668-6484.

Washtenaw Cycling & Fitness, 3400 Washtenaw Ave., Ann Arbor; ☎ (313) 971-2121.

Bike Haus, 9977 E. Grand River, Brighton; ☎ (313) 227-5070.

Town & Country Cyclery, 8160 W. Grand River, Brighton; ☎ (313) 227-4420.

Village Cyclery, 109 E. Main St., Pinckney; ☎ (313) 878-0117.

Area attractions

Bentley Historical Library, Ann Arbor; ☎ (313) 764-3482.

Clements Library, Ann Arbor; ☎ (313) 764-2347.

Cobblestone Farm, Ann Arbor; ☎ (313) 994-2928.

Hands-On Museum, Ann Arbor; ☎ (313) 995-5439.

Kelsey Museum of Archeology, Ann Arbor; ☎ (313) 764-9309.

Kempf House, Ann Arbor; ☎ (313) 994-4898.

Leslie Science Center, Ann Arbor; ☎ (313) 662-7802.

Margaret Dow Towsley Sports Museum, Schembechler Hall, Ann Arbor; ☎ (313) 747-2583.

Matthaei Botanical Gardens, Ann Arbor; ☎ (313) 998-7061.

Museum of Art, Ann Arbor; ☎ (313) 764-0395.

Nichols Arboretum, Ann Arbor (trails for walking or bicycling).

Ruthven Exhibit Museum, Ann Arbor; ☎ (313) 764-0478.

Spring Valley Trout Farm, Dexter; ☎ (313) 426-4772.

Area events and festivals

March: Ann Arbor Film Festival, Ann Arbor Flower and Garden Show, Ann Arbor; Pioneer Craft Fair, Dexter.

April: Ann Arbor Antiques Market (all summer), Winefest, Ann Arbor Spring Art Fair, Ann Arbor.

May: Gus Macker 3-on-3 Basketball Tournament, Ann Arbor.

June: Ann Arbor Summer Festival.

July: Huron River Day, Ann Arbor Art Fair, Ann Arbor.

August: Heritage Festival, Ypsilanti; Ann Arbor Antiques Market, Country Peddler Craft Show, Ann Arbor.

September: Weekends at Wiard Orchards, Ypsilanti; Saline Community Fair; Ann Arbor Blues & Jazz Festival.

October: Apple Days, Dexter; Super Fest (music), Ann Arbor; Ann Arbor Winter Air Fair.

Travel information

Ann Arbor Area Convention & Visitors Bureau, 120 West Huron, Ann Arbor, MI 48104; ☎ (313) 995-7281.

City of Ann Arbor Bicycle Program, Department of Parks and Recreation, City Hall, P.O. Box 8647, Ann Arbor, MI 48107; ☎ (313) 994-2786.

Cyclists pause at the Sharon Mills Winery in the Ann Arbor area, the highlight of Bike Tour 4.

Winery Tour

Trip Card

Starting point: Ann Arbor
County: Washtenaw
Distance: 55 miles
Shorter option: 24 miles
Terrain: moderately hilly
Highlights: Manchester, Sharon Mills Winery, rolling countryside
Suggested riders: intermediate

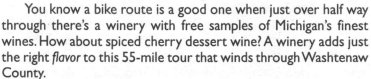

You know a bike route is a good one when just over half way through there's a winery with free samples of Michigan's finest wines. How about spiced cherry dessert wine? A winery adds just the right *flavor* to this 55-mile tour that winds through Washtenaw County.

The route, designed by the Ann Arbor Touring and Biking Society, uses carefully chosen roads with plenty of fun, rolling hills to keep you interested. The roads on this route travel southwest of Ann Arbor past an array of country scenery: classic red barns, hillsides filled with sheep and fields of corn. Of course, any route starting in Ann Arbor offers plenty of activities and food choices afterwards for you and your cycling buddies.

For almost 40 years, folks have ventured to Manchester in Washtenaw County's southwest corner to savor the taste of the Manchester Chicken Broil each July. The River Raisin winds through this quaint town, the starting point for the shorter option. There are also orchards nearby and plenty of eateries and antique shops in Manchester besides the town's picturesque mill.

Stage one (9.6 miles) Start at Wheeler Park, located on the corner of Depot and North Fourth avenues (just north of downtown Ann Arbor). Head south on North Fourth and cycle through the intersection of Beakes Street. You will pass the Kerrytown shops on your left. This trio of restored buildings houses a collection of shops and unique restaurants. The Kerrytown Shops are open seven days a week while a Farmer's Market is set up on Wednesday and Saturday and an Artisans Market on Sunday.

Beakes Street can be a congested road, but more so in the middle of the week than on weekends (unless there is a U of M football game, of course). Turn right (west) onto East Liberty in a half mile where you'll quickly cross the busy intersection at Main Street. You'll cycle for about three miles on Liberty Street as you make your way out of Ann Arbor. Use caution as you journey through the traffic light at Seventh Street at **Mile 1.3**. There are some hills on Liberty Street along with a mixture of sidewalks and gravel shoulders.

At **Mile 2.2**, you'll cross West Stadium, a busy intersection, and then make your way up a hill. After Liberty Street climbs over I-94, the road narrows to two lanes. You'll cross the Wagner Road intersection before switching gears and climbing a hill that curves to your right at **Mile 3.7**.

Within a mile you'll enjoy the shade of a long, forested downhill stretch. At **Mile 5.5** you turn left (south) onto Zeeb Road, a hilly, two-lane road with gravel shoulders. You'll pass a classic red barn before you turn right (west) on Scio Church Road at **Mile 6.5**. This forested road is one of those soothing country rides that cyclists dream about during a hectic work week. The Salem Lutheran Church with its cemetery is at **Mile 8.6**, followed by cornfields, cows, farms and more barns. Before you turn left (south) onto Parker Road, you might want to stop and catch your breath before beginning the next leg to Manchester.

Stage two (15 miles) Parker Road is a straight, north-south road that is ideal for picking up the speed before you have to climb some fairly steep hills when the road curves to the right and becomes Pleasant Lake Road. There are more rolling hills and country scenery along Pleasant Lake Road, which has gravel shoulders. The road winds through a pair of curves and it is important

WHEELER PARK

Start • 0 Miles
Finish • 55 Miles
Short loop 24 Miles

Fourth Ave.

N

ANN ARBOR

Liberty

SHARON MILLS
WINERY TOUR

6.5 Miles

Zeeb

Scio Church

12

45.1 Miles

Pleasant Lake

15 Miles

Austin

94

Haist   Fletcher

Austin

52

Pleasant Lake

MANCHESTER

25 Miles

30.1 Miles

Sharon Hollow Rd.

to stay to the right at the second curve and *NOT* follow the paved road to the left.

Turn left (south) onto Schneider Road at **Mile 15** and then climb the first of several hills. Schneider Road is a favorite of the Ann Arbor Touring & Biking Society because of its rolling hills and light traffic.

A very long uphill section is reached at **Mile 15.8** and within a mile you come to the intersection of Bethel Church Road, where you'll find the Bethel Church, a charming stone structure with an adjacent cemetery. Just past the church, you can really pick up the speed without much effort as it's mostly downhill with a few dips. Turn right (west) onto Austin Road at **Mile 18.2**. A bumpy road at first, Austin winds through rolling hills, where at times you can enjoy an almost panoramic view of the countryside.

After passing through a residential area, the road curves to the right and then climbs uphill to reach M-52 at **Mile 23.5**. You briefly follow M-52 to cross the River Raisin in a quarter mile, and the state highway curves north while you remain on City Road to arrive in Manchester. Turn left (west) onto Main Street at **Mile 24.6** to reach the business district of the village.

The town's historic mill is on the left and now houses antique shops. There are some food choices in town, including a bakery and a deli. Haarer's Meeting Place at 223 E. Main Street offers healthy home cooking.

Stage three (5.3 miles) Continue west out of Manchester along Main Street. Just beyond the business district is Carr Park with picnic tables, a pavilion and a vault toilet.

Turn right (north) onto Sharon Hollow Road at **Mile 27.5** where you're able to enjoy a downhill stretch to the winery. The road winds through a pair of curves past sheep farms and then a jogs briefly along Sharon Valley Road at **Mile 29** before continuing north. Now you can fly effortlessly down a hill right into the Sharon Mills Winery.

There's no charge for wine tasting at the winery, which opens at noon Saturdays and Sundays. Even if you're not a wine sampler, the grounds and the historic structure make it a natural place for a break.

The Sharon Mills Winery is the oldest of the village industry

The Sharon Mills Winery near Manchester, a place to stop for a fine bottle of Michigan-produced wine. (Photo by Ken Bawcom)

mills owned by Henry Ford. The Greek Revival structure, built in 1834, was operated by the Ford Motor Company from 1939 to 1951, and produced cigar lighters, using recycled metal. The building was a private residence for 30 years and was then transformed into a winery. While the generator provides power to produce wine, the cool, stone-walled basement of the mill is used for aging champagne.

Don't go overboard on the wine samples, as you still have 25 miles to go!

Stage four (25 miles) From the winery, you head north along Sharon Hollow Road up a hill (hope you didn't buy too many bottles of wine!). The road curves uphill and becomes Pleasant Lake Road at *Mile 30*. Pleasant Lake Road levels out and heads straight east through scenic, open country. Near the corner of M-52 at *Mile 33.5*, there's a small store for quick energy boosters followed by the Salem Church. Continue straight on Pleasant Lake Road, past a small airport and more hills, and eventually you reach Fletcher Road at *Mile 36.8*. Turn left (north) on this road that is another favorite of the local bike club.

Near *Mile 40* Fletcher Road winds through a pair of curves.

In less than a mile you turn right (east) onto Scio Church Road. After passing some small lakes, you cross Parker Road at *Mile 45* then backtrack to Ann Arbor the same way you came. You'll make your way up some hills that are steeper than they appear to be before reaching the four-way stop sign at Zeeb Road. Ann Arbor is entered at *Mile 51.4*. Turn left (north) onto Seventh Street, then right (east) onto Liberty Street at *Mile 53.7* where you'll encounter a bike lane.

The road goes downhill through the Third Street intersection at *Mile 54* and then uphill through the Ashley Street intersection. Cross Main Street before turning left onto Fourth Street and at *Mile 55* you're back at your starting point in Wheeler Park.

Shorter option (24 miles) To shorten this route, begin in the business district of Manchester and head west on Main Street. Turn right (north) onto Sharon Hollow Road, right (east) onto Pleasant Lake Road and make another right (south) on Schneider Road. Finally turn right (west) onto Austin Road to return to Manchester. By beginning and ending in Manchester, you'll still be able to make a stop at the winery as well as follow some of the favorite roads of the Ann Arbor Touring & Biking Society.

Bicycle service, sales

Cycle Cellar, 220 Felch, Ann Arbor; ☎ (313) 769-1115.

Student Bike Shop, 607 S. Forest, Ann Arbor; ☎ (313) 662-6986.

Ann Arbor Cyclery, 1224 Packard, Ann Arbor; ☎ (313) 761-2749.

Campus Bike & Toy Center, 514 E. William, Ann Arbor; ☎ (313) 662-0035.

Great Lakes Fitness & Cycling, 560 S. Main St., Ann Arbor; ☎ (313) 668-6484.

Washtenaw Cycling & Fitness, 3400 Washtenaw Ave., Ann Arbor; ☎ (313) 971-2121.

Area attractions

Sharon Mills Winery; ☎ (313) 428-9160 (see Huron River Ramble for more Ann Arbor attractions).

Area events and festivals

March: Ann Arbor Film Festival, Ann Arbor Flower and Garden Show, Ann Arbor; Pioneer Craft Fair, Dexter.

April: Ann Arbor Antiques Market (all summer), Winefest, Ann Arbor Spring Art Fair, Ann Arbor.

June: Ann Arbor Summer Festival.

July: Huron River Day, Ann Arbor Art Fair, Ann Arbor; Manchester Chicken Broil, Manchester.

August: Heritage Festival, Ypsilanti; Ann Arbor Antiques Market, Country Peddler Craft Show, Ann Arbor.

September: Weekends at Wiard Orchards, Ypsilanti; Saline Community Fair, Saline; Ann Arbor Blues & Jazz Festival, Ann Arbor.

October: Apple Days, Dexter; Super Fest (music), Ann Arbor; Ann Arbor Winter Art Fair.

Travel information

Ann Arbor Convention & Visitors Bureau, 120 West Huron, Ann Arbor, MI 48104; ☎ (313) 995-7281.

City of Ann Arbor Bicycle Program, Department of Parks and Recreation, City Hall, P.O. Box 8647, Ann Arbor, MI 48107; ☎ (313) 994-2786.

Manchester Community Resource Center; ☎ (313) 428-7722.

Cycling Trip Tip #4

If a spoke breaks, stop right away and remove it completely from the wheel or at the very least twist it around the spoke next to it. A flapping rear-wheel spoke can jam the rear derailleur and cause a serious mishap.

Kensington Metropark makes for an ideal family outing, combining a bike path with a trip around Kent Lake in a park setting.

Kensington Tour

Trip Card

Starting point: Kensington Metropark
Counties: Livingston, Oakland
Distance: 8 miles
Terrain: flat to small rolling hills
Highlights: Wildwing Lake, Kent Lake, nature center
Suggested riders: beginners

In 1940, voters in five counties approved a special millage for a special park district called the Huron-Clinton Metropolitan Authority. Today the authority operates 13 metroparks throughout the region. The popular parks offer an array of amenities and activities including golf, canoeing, camping, hiking, cross country skiing, nature study, in-line skating, sledding and playground facilities.

But best of all, 8 out of the 13 parks include 10-foot wide paved biking (and hiking) trails, away from the pitfalls of automobile traffic. Kensington Metropark, with 8 miles of bike paths, is one of the most popular parks. Here the bike trails are clearly marked - a wonderful place for families and groups who want a leisurely ride that winds, twists and dips through an area of lakes, marshes, trees, fields and orchards. And, ah yes, it's close to home to the 4.3 million of you in Southeast Michigan.

The bike paths aren't totally flat which adds to the fun. There are some moderate hills to climb and some downhill slopes to pick up momentum. The paths journey through many shaded, wooded areas, over bridges and by open areas where you can see off into the distance. With all that Kensington Metropark has to offer, a cycling excursion can be easily combined with a family reunion or a leisurely afternoon on the water.

Many special events take place at the Kensington Metropark at the Nature Center or at the Farm Center, including a Fall Festival, a Spring Festival and a Country Fair. The park is also the site of the annual M.S. Fall Breakaway, an organized bike tour with routes of 25, 50 and 75 miles as well as an 18-mile mountain bike route. Kensington Metropark is located just off I-96 and reached by departing at exit 151 and following the signs.

Entrance fees: A Metroparks vehicle entry permit and registration are required for all programs. Current entry permit charges are $2 per vehicle on weekdays, $3 on weekends, Tuesdays free. Annual passes can also be purchased for $15 at any metropark or by contacting the administrative offices of the metroparks at: 1300 High Ridge Dr., P.O. Box 2001, Brighton, MI 48116; ☎ (800) 47-PARKS. Other metroparks with paved bike trails include: Metro Beach, Stony Creek, Indian Springs, Hudson Mills, Lower Huron, Oakwoods and Willow.

Stage one (3.5 miles) Park at the West Boat Launch Area, past the toll booth, where the bike trails are clearly visible from the parking lot. Hop on! With Kent Lake to your right (east) and Wildwing Lake to your left (west) head north in a clockwise direction to arrive at the Nature Center and foot trails in a quarter mile. The bike trail winds past the center and more views of the water and the woods. There are some hills in the first mile and lots of picnic tables and benches along the way. At a stop sign at **Mile 1.6** you cross Island Road, which leads south to five picnic areas including two (Flagstaff and Turtlehead) on an island. The park has a total of 15 picnic areas, and eight of which have shelters, including Baywoods which is passed after crossing Island Road.

A long gradual uphill stretch is encountered at **Mile 2** and within a half mile you reach a scenic vantage point above Kent Lake. Make a sharp left across the street at **Mile 2.6** and then a fun downhill stretch will lead you near the water. The Farm Cen-

ter and Food Bar will be to your left at **Mile 3.5**. At the hands-on farm center, children and adults are invited to learn by touching and exploring. You can walk down the farm lanes, view the animals and take in the activities of a working farm. It's also the place for hayrides and sleigh rides on weekends. The Food Bar is located in a turn-of-the-century farm house and has pop and ice cream.

    Stage two (4.5 miles) Continuing on the trail in a clockwise direction, you'll pass by an open area as you curve left down a hill which is followed by a few more rolling hills at **Mile 5**. The trail follows a sidewalk briefly before making a a sharp left at **Mile 5.5**. Just follow the bike path signs.

    There's a picnic pavilion at Martindale Beach at **Mile 6** followed by a portion of the trail that parallels the highway. At **Mile**

Among the wildlife that can be seen at Kensington Metropark are swans, residents of Kent Lake.

6.6 you cross over a wooden bridge.

As the trail parallels I-96, you cross over another wooden structure at **Mile 7.2**, a nice place to stop and enjoy a view of the lake. The final leg begins with a downhill that curves into a scenic stretch along the Kent Lake shore before ending at the West Boat Launch parking lot at Mile 8. Time to take in that craft demonstration, lay around by the water or grill that chicken.

Bicycle sales, service

Bike Haus, 9977 E. Grand River, Brighton; ☎ (810) 227-5070.

Town & Country Cyclery, 8160 W. Grand River, Brighton; ☎(810) 227-4420.

D&D Bicycles, 121 N. Center Northville; ☎ (810)347-1511.

Town & Country Cyclery, 148 N. Center, Northville; ☎ (810) 349-7140.

Jerry's Bicycles, 1449 W. Ann Arbor, Plymouth; ☎ (810) 459-1500.

Plymouth Trading Post Bicycle Shop, 1009 W. Ann Arbor, Plymouth; ☎ (810) 453-5130.

Town & Country Cyclery, 141 E. Lake, Walled Lake; ☎ (810) 960-9190.

Pro Cycle Center, 41766 Ten Mile, Novi; ☎ (810) 646-7565.

Cycle & Fitness USA, 39600 W. 14 Mile, Novi; ☎ (810) 960-1371.

Village Cyclery, 109 E. Main St., Pinckney; ☎ (313) 878-0117.

Area events, festivals

April-May: Spring Festival, Kensington Metropark.

July: County Fair, Kensington Metropark.

August: Folk Art Festival, Brighton.

September: MS Fall Breakaway, Kensington Metropark.

Travel information

Kensington Metropark; ☎ (810) 685-1561.

Huron-Clinton Metropolitan Authority; ☎ (810) 227-2757.

Brighton Area Chamber of Commerce; ☎ (810) 227-5086.

Paint Creek Trail was the first rail trail developed in Michigan.

6

Paint Creek Trail

Trip Card

Starting point: Rochester
County: Oakland
Distance: 24 miles
Shorter option: 6 miles
Terrain: Flat
Highlights: Rail-trail, cider mills, U-pick
farms, Paint Creek
Suggested Riders: Beginners and intermediate

Paint Creek was the first rail-trail project to open in Michigan, a state that is now crisscrossed with such avenues for cyclists and hikers. But while now there may be many others, few, if any, are as popular as the original rail-trail.

On any pleasant weekend from spring through fall Paint Creek Trail is a busy route with the vast majority of users being cyclists. Its popularity is due to both scenery and location. The trail spans 8 miles from Rochester to Lake Orion in an area of Oakland County that is being ruled by bulldozers as subdivisions, strip malls and pizza parlors pop up like mushrooms in the spring.

Yet despite all this *development*, at times Paint Creek Trail is a wooded path that touches ponds, marshlands, grassy meadows and Paint Creek itself, a gurgling trout stream that looks like it belongs in northern Michigan. Being a former corridor of the Penn Central Line, there is also an occasional railroad artifact along the route, including rails, wooden ties and even communications boxes. More important to some people, the trail, due to its railroad heritage, is flat with a surprisingly gradual incline despite the fact that you gain more than 300 feet traveling from the Clinton River in Rochester to Lake Orion.

Like many other rail-trails, Paint Creek's surface is a crushed slag better suited for mountain and hybrid bikes than it is for road bikes. The rest of this 23.5-mile loop follows paved roads with the exception of a mile along Snell Road, which is hard-packed dirt.

Pack a lunch. The trail features numerous bridges over the creek and even terraced steps down to the water where it's pleasant to sit and rest for a spell. Or else pack a basket. The loop's second half winds through farm country past numerous U-pick berry farms and farmer's markets.

Unlike the LakeLands Trail that is maintained as a state park, there are no fees for Paint Creek. The trail officially begins in a unit of the Rochester-Utica Recreation Area on Avon Road, 1.5 miles southeast of Rochester. But the rail-trail is interrupted along the way so the best place to start this ride is at Rochester Municipal Park. To reach the park, depart M-59 at Rochester Road and head north. In downtown Rochester, Rochester Road becomes Main Street and here you turn west on Third Street and then north on Pine Street to reach the park in three blocks.

Stage one (8.5 miles) Rochester Municipal Park is a maze of sidewalks, play equipment and picnic tables. Paint Creek flows through the middle of the park and the trail follows its northeast side. The easiest place to pick it up, however, is where Ludlow Road crosses the creek at the northernmost point of the park. Here the trail is well posted on both sides of the road.

Heading north, you quickly cross Paint Creek and then arrive at a stairway that leads into the foot trail system of Dinosaur Hill Nature Preserve. Named after a hill that children thought looked like a sleeping brontosaurus, the 16-acre nature center includes a handful of short trails and a small but pleasant interpretive center. Call (810) 656-0999 for hours if you plan to stop.

From the preserve the trail arrives at Tienken Road within

a third of a mile and then at **Mile 1.5** crosses the creek a second time where just beyond the bridge is a series of steps leading down to the water. Dutton Road is the next road the trail crosses and at **Mile 2.5** it reaches Silver Bell Road. In between, you cross several bridges over Paint Creek and pass several bends of the stream that have been stabilized by a local Trout Unlimited Chapter with logs, rocks and wire mesh. The state has since planted rainbow trout in Paint Creek and some natural reproduction even takes place now. Ride the route in May and June and you're bound to see a few anglers tossing worms into the creek to entice the trout.

In the next half mile you pass several views of the creek and another series of steps along the bank before reaching Gallagher

Road at **Mile 3** in the historic hamlet of Goodison. The first mill was built here in 1835 and since has been replaced with the one that is seen from the trail. Today Paint Creek Cider Mill is a noted restaurant that also sells ice cream and homemade cider from September through Christmas. Follow Orion Road a short ways north and you'll reach Goodison Cider Mill, the other one in town.

Back on the rail trail and heading north, you pass a handful of impressive homes to the east, some with their own ponds, and wetlands to the west. Here Paint Creek itself is nowhere in sight as it flows through nearby private property.

At **Mile 3.5** you cross Gunn Road and reach Adams Road in another mile. Just beyond Adams you pass the Royal Oak Archery Club. You're safe, but still the sight of those target bales definitely makes you pick up the pace. Paint Creek returns a quarter mile from the club and stays in sight for the next half mile.

You finally cross to the west side of the creek on a bridge at **Mile 5.5** and soon break out of the hardwood forest at the intersection of Kern and Clarkston Road, high above the rushing water. The trail is now passing through a small parcel of the Bald Mountain Recreation Area; just beyond Clarkston Road are the last set of stairs leading down to the water.

At **Mile 8** you enter Lake Orion and arrive at an ORV barrier for ORVs across the trail. Here you can depart the rail-trail and continue north on Newton Drive to reach Atwater Road in a quarter mile. Or if you're hungry, pass through the posts and follow the trail to its north end.

Paint Creek Trail actually terminates at the parking lot for the LS Family Foods shopping center, where the supermarket has a deli. There's also a Tastee Freez in the complex for soft serve ice cream. Nearby are Wendy's, Marco's for pizza and Cooke's Dairy Farm Ice Cream (a local brand) or Brian's Restaurant, a pleasant place where you can sit for a spell.

Stage two (12.5 miles) The shopping center is on the corner of M-24 and Atwater Road. Head east on Atwater to pass

On the Paint Creek Rail-Trail, cyclists share the former railroad bed with equestrians and walkers.

Newton Drive and within a block you'll come to Perry Road where on the corner is Atwater Park. Turn left (north) on Perry and follow it until it ends at E. Flint Road. Turn right (east) on E. Flint and at **Mile 9.8** you arrive at a stop sign where E. Flint splits into Miller Road and Orion Road. Head right (south) on Orion. This is a paved road with gravel shoulders and moderate traffic that will lead you out of Lake Orion.

At **Mile 10.7** you turn left (east) on Stoney Creek Road, well paved with gravel shoulders and less traffic. To the right are homes but to the left is Bald Mountain Recreation Area, the second time you've passed through this 4,637-acre state park unit. Within a half mile you'll pass a green gate and a trail on the state park side of the road. Follow the trail a short ways and you'll end up at the top of the best sledding hill in northern Oakland County, with a scenic view of a pair of lakes.

You pass the junction with Adams Road and then immediately arrive at Harmon Road at **Mile 12**. For the best view of this state park, head north on Harmon, a dirt road. This is mountain biking country and within a half mile you come to the parking area overlooking Heart Lake, where the park's White Loop passes through. Turn right (east) on nearby Predmore Road and in another quarter mile you arrive at the posted Graham Lake and the Graham Lakes Trailhead.

Retreat to Stoney Creek Road and turn left (east). At **Mile 14.2**, you pass delightful Middleton Berry Farm with its rows of raspberries and strawberries and bright red farm buildings. In another third of a mile, Stoney Creek Road curves to the right (south) while departing to the north is Lake George Road, a dirt road. At **Mile 15** Stoney Creek Road curves to the left (east).

When it straightens out, Stoney Creek is a pleasant ride past farm fields, barns and other rural scenery. The road has a roll to it as you climb over a series of low hills which provide a rare glimpse of Oakland County's farm country. Are the days of this rural postcard numbered? Probably. Already marring this simple scenery is a golf course and a new subdivision.

At *Mile 17*, Stoney Creek ends at the junction with Rochester Road. Turn right (south) on Rochester, paved and with wide gravel shoulders and considerably more traffic. Within a mile and half you arrive at a long downhill stretch, followed by an equally long climb. Once at the top you can swing into Foolers U-pick Farm and Market for a break. The open-air market is open from 10 a.m. to 6 p.m. most of the year and along with fruit and vegetables, sells cider when in season.

You depart Rochester Road at *Mile 19.5* at its intersection with Snell Road. Turn right (west) on Snell, a hard packed and oiled road that road bikes can easily handle. It's also a scenic road, winding past woods and Pine Row Farm's impressive barn, and then in a mile, finishing off with a long downhill segment.

You bottom out at the corner of Snell and Orion Road and by heading right (north) for a quarter mile you pass Paint Creek Cider Mill for the second time and re-enter Goodison at *Mile 21*.

Stage three (3 miles) The final stage is a return to Rochester Municipal Park via the Paint Creek Trail. Pick up the rail-trail where it crosses the creek adjacent to the Paint Creek Cider Mill and head south along its most scenic stretch. You will reach the city park in 3 miles to finish off this 24-mile loop. If you're hungry and thirsty after the ride, there are many restaurants and cafes to choose from in downtown Rochester. After a ride, I like to hit the soda fountain counter at Knapp's Dairy Bar or have a cold brew and hamburger at Mr. B's Pub.

Shorter Option (6 miles) The first 3 miles of the Paint Creek Trail makes a round-trip of 6 miles that's excellent for families with children as they can break up the ride with stops at Dinosaur Hill Nature Center or a cider mill.

Bicycle sales, service
Kinetic Systems, 60 S. Main St., Clarkston; ☎ (810) 625-7000.
King's Bikes, 425 Main St., Rochester; ☎ (810) 651-4277.

MGM Bicycle & Fitness Equipment, 2680 S. Rochester, Rochester Hills; ☎ (810) 852-0888.

Sterling Schwinn, 878 S. Rochester, Rochester Hills; ☎(810) 652-1555.

Orion Bicycle, 1150 S. Lapeer, Lake Orion; ☎ (810) 693-3333.

Scarlett's Schwinn Cyclery, 203 N. Perry, Pontiac; ☎ (810) 333-7843.

Tom Nell Bicycles, 2528 Elizabeth Lake, Pontiac; ☎ (810) 682-5456.

Town & Country Cyclery, 3722 Elizabeth Lake, Waterford; ☎ (810) 681-8600.

Area Attractions

Yates Cider Mill, Rochester; ☎ (810) 651-8300.

Rochester Hills Museum, Rochester Hills; ☎ (810) 656-4663.

Meadow Brook Hall, Rochester; ☎ (810) 370-3140.

Middleton Berry Farm, Lake Orion; ☎ (810) 693-6018.

Area Events And Festivals

May: Heritage Festival, Rochester.

August: International Art Fair, Rochester.

September: Apples and Arts Festival, Rochester.

Travel information

Rochester Chamber of Commerce; ☎ (810) 651-6700.

Bald Mountain Recreation Area; ☎ (810) 693-6767.

Cycling Trip Tip #5

When riding you can't drink too much water. But it's important to drink, not gulp, and to begin drinking before you feel thirsty because the sensation of dehydration always lags behind your body's actual need for liquids. Make it a habit to drink from your water bottle no less than four times an hour. Want to improve the flavor of your water? Add a small amount of lemon or fruit juice to it.

7

The Lakes Loop

Trip Card

Starting point: Oxford
Counties: Oakland, Genesee and Lapeer
Distance: 57 miles
Shorter options: 24 and 6 miles
Terrain: hilly
Highlights: State parks, lakes, cider mills
Suggested Riders: Intermediate to advanced

Southern Oakland County seems like an endless sea of strip malls, shopping centers, subdivisions, fast food chains and other forms of development lurching out of control like a run-away bulldozer. Northern Oakland County is a charming area of fruit farms and cider mills, small towns with millponds, many parks, hills and lots of lakes.

Some day, but hopefully not in my lifetime, one region of the county will overrun the other. It's inevitable but until it does cyclists can enjoy this 57-mile Lakes Loop, a delightful ride through rural scenery and quaint villages that is remarkably close to home for anybody living in Flint or metropolitan Detroit.

This ride is not for beginners. It's 57 miles long and much of the route is hilly. Not gut-busters, but you are constantly changing gears in the kind of broken terrain that many of cyclists enjoy and others find tiring. There is also a 5-mile stretch along a hard packed dirt road and brief stretches of Dixie Highway and M-15 that can be moderately busy with traffic at times.

The attractions of the Lakes Loop, however, are clearly worth putting up with a busy stretch of road. This route journeys pass two state parks, including three miles into Holly Recreation Area. There are two cider mills along the way if you're riding in late summer, a U-pick-it berry farm if it's early summer and hardwood forests if you arrive during fall colors.

Most of all, there are lakes, ponds and scenic marshes. There are more than a dozen named lakes along this route, more that are unnamed, as well as ponds, rivers and streams that connect them. Three parks along water serve as convenient rest stops between stages.

I like to begin this loop in Oxford, a delightful small town located on M-24 (Lapeer Road), 16 miles south of I-69 at exit 155, or 10 miles north of I-75 from exit 81. There's plenty of parking in its downtown area as well as an interesting little museum and several places to chow down after the long ride.

Stage One (19.2 miles) The heart of downtown Oxford is the intersection of M-24 and Burdick Road, where on the corner is the Northeast Oakland Historic Museum, housed in an old bank. Heading west you'll pedal past several mansions and other older homes to quickly leave the village where Burdick becomes Seymour Lake Road. At **Mile 1.5**, you pass your first lake, actually a series of them. The one you see to the left is Tan Lake, the glimpse of one to the north is of Whipple Lake. At **Mile 3**, you pass Oxford Township Park and in a half mile you reach a stop sign.

Seymour Lake Road ends at M-15 but along the way makes three turns at intersections before getting there. It is well marked as *Seymour Lake Road*, however, and features wide gravel shoulders and moderate traffic. At the stop sign turn left (south) to briefly join Baldwin Road and then in 0.4 mile turn right (west). At **Mile 4.6** you turn left (south) again to stay with the pavement.

Seymour Lake Road now straightens out and passes another lake before you arrive at a 4-way stop sign with Sashabaw Road at

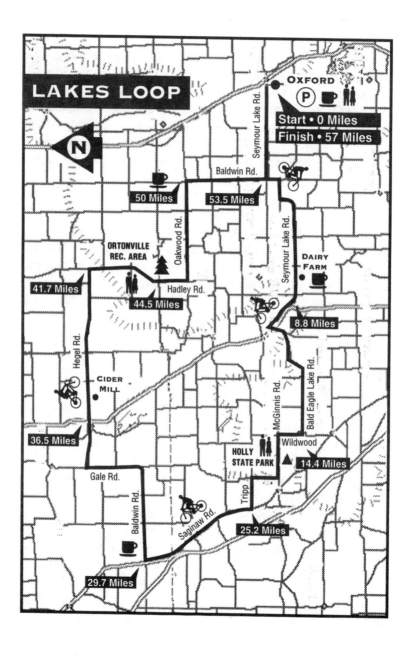

LAKES LOOP

N

OXFORD

Start • 0 Miles
Finish • 57 Miles

Seymour Lake Rd.

Baldwin Rd.

50 Miles

53.5 Miles

Oakwood Rd.

ORTONVILLE
REC. AREA

Seymour Lake Rd.

DAIRY
FARM

41.7 Miles

Hadley Rd.

44.5 Miles

8.8 Miles

Hegel Rd.

CIDER
MILL

Bald Eagle Lake Rd.

McGinnis Rd.

36.5 Miles

Wildwood

HOLLY
STATE PARK

14.4 Miles

Gale Rd.

Baldwin Rd.

Tripp

Saginaw Rd.

25.2 Miles

29.7 Miles

Mile 6.2. Just on the other side of the intersection is Ashton Orchards, which sells fruit and cider. But if you're hungry, wait! There's a better place just down the road. After pedaling past Seymour Lake itself, you arrive at Cook's Dairy Farm at *Mile 6.7*.

This is a local hot spot for ice cream lovers. They make deliciously rich ice cream that can be enjoyed in cones, a cup, as a hot fudge sundae or milk shake. You can sit and relax at picnic tables out front, or do as the locals do, wander in the back and enjoy your cone while feeding grass to the dairy cows. Are we in the country or what?

Seymour Lake Road continues west, passing signs of the advancing suburbs, and at *Mile 8.8* arrives at M-15 (Ortonville Road). Turn right (north) and be careful! This can be a busy road at times but it features wide shoulders that are partially paved. Plus you only have to stay on it for 1.2 miles. After passing Huff Lake and Lake Louise to your right, turn left (south) on Allen Road at *Mile 10*. It's posted, but watch for the street sign as it's easy to miss the road.

Allen Road heads south but within a half mile you veer off to the right (west) onto Bald Eagle Lake Road which skirts the shore of Bald Eagle Lake. This is a pretty lakeshore stretch that ends when the pavement ends at *Mile 10.8*. For the next 5 miles you will be on a hard packed dirt road. It is much better suited for hybrid or mountain bikes but the surface is so well graded and maintained that road bikes can usually handle it without too many problems. Besides, Bald Eagle Lake Road is a delightful pedal of wide curves, gentle hills and lakes, much of it in a shaded forest.

At *Mile 12.4*, you pass through the intersection with Bird Road and a mile later you arrive at a stop sign at Jossan Road. Stay on Bald Eagle Lake Road as it moves out of the woods and passes a handful of farms and cornfields. At *Mile 14.4* Bald Eagle Lake Road ends at the "T" intersection with Wildwood, another dirt road. Turn right (north) for a mile and then turn left (west) on McGinnis Road at *Mile 15.5*. McGinnis begins as a dirt road but within a half mile turns to pleasant pavement, and at that point

One of the highlights of the Lakes Tour is a stop at Cook's Dairy Farm for homemade ice cream and to feed the cows.

you turn left (south) into the first of two state parks.

This is the entrance to the Heron and Wildwood Lakes day-use area of Holly Recreation Area. Being on a bicycle, a non-motorized means of transportation, you don't have to pay an entry fee. The park road here is 3 miles long and a fun ride; and it climbs and descends a number of hills as it makes its away around Heron, Valley and finally Wildwood Lakes. Along the way there are seven picnic areas. Scenic Overlook Area is less than a mile from the entrance and features a pavilion, water and an overview of the

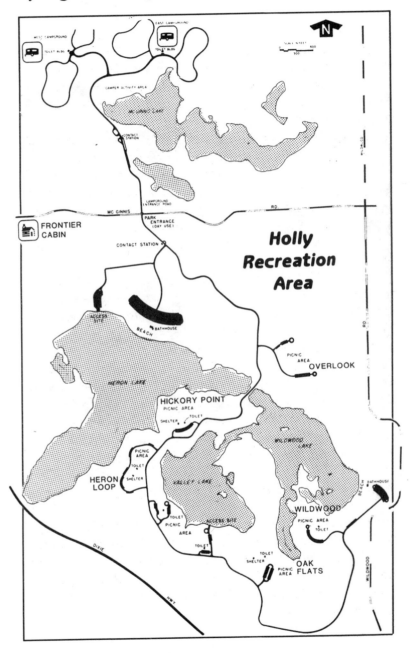

park.

From there you descend rapidly to pass between Heron and Wildwood Lakes and then climb to Hickory Point Picnic Area (tables, toilets, pavilion, water). The park road ends at Wildwood Beach Area where there are more tables, water, a bathhouse and a swimming area to cool you off after completing this 19.2-mile stage of the ride.

Stage two (17.3 miles) Backtrack out of the park to the entrance of the day-use area and at McGinnis Road turn left (west). Within a mile you'll arrive at a stop sign. Turn right (north) on Van Road, which features wide, paved shoulders and light traffic. You'll pass Groveland County Park, another popular campground in this area, and then at **Mile 24.2** come to a stop sign at the intersection with Tripp Road. Van Road continues north here as a dirt road. You turn left (west) and follow Tripp Road, which is paved.

At **Mile 25.2**, you arrive at Dixie Highway. It may seem strange to be cycling a four-lane road like Dixie but it has extremely wide shoulders that are partially paved and, thanks to I-75 which parallels it here, only moderate traffic most of the time. Still, you have to use some caution following it for the next 4.5 miles.

Turn right (north) on Dixie to immediately pass a mountain...Mt. Holly that is, Oakland County's popular downhill ski area. Within 1.5 miles you pass the entrance to the Michigan Renaissance Festival. If this ride is taking place on a weekend in August through September, this patch of woods and fields will be filled with kings and queens, court jesters and Shakespearean actors. Plan to pull in for a while if your timing is right as it is a wonderful event where you can sit around gnawing on a turkey leg while watching Hamlet.

In another mile, you pass the entrance point to I-75, but signs here keep you on Dixie Highway as you enter Lapeer County. You finally depart Dixie Highway at **Mile 29.7** when you reach Baldwin Road. On the corner is a gas station and a convenience store to restock the saddle bags. Turn right (east) on Baldwin and leave the four lanes and traffic behind.

In the beginning, Baldwin is a newly paved surface with wide gravel shoulders and light traffic. You immediately move into the country, where you pass several farms, including a horse farm, and at **Mile 32.2** arrive at Symanzik's Berry Farm. The U-pick-it farm specializes in strawberries and raspberries and has a small playground/picnic area to relax in.

Continue on Baldwin and in another mile it curves left (north) and merges into Gale Road. At **Mile 35.2**, you arrive at a stop sign where on the corner is Goodrich High School. Turn right (east) on Hegel Road, another newly paved surface with wide shoulders, to quickly enter the hamlet of Goodrich.

In the heart of this village, reached at **Mile 36.5** of the route, is a millpond and, across the street, Goodrich Commons. The walk-in park features picnic tables overlooking a shaded stream, a pavilion and vault toilets. Nearby, on the corner of Hegel and M-15, are two convenience stores. If you rather take an extended break at a cider mill, continued the ride for another 1.6 miles.

Stage Three (8.5 miles) From the intersection of Hegel and M-15, turn left (north) on the busy state highway but then make an immediate right (east) turn back on Hegel to escape the traffic. At **Mile 38**, you come to Porter's Orchard and Cider Mill that sells the sweet juice and apples when in season, along with peaches and other produce. Outside the mill, there is a small fenced-in picnic area with a handful of tables.

Once past the cider mill Hegel Road becomes very hilly as it winds past a handful of ponds, marshes and even a small lake. The hills end when Hegel does, at the "T" intersection with Hadley Road at **Mile 41.7**. Turn right (south) on Hadley, a newly paved road with narrow shoulders but light traffic. It's another hilly ride through more rural scenery until **Mile 44.5**, the entrance to the Big Fish Lake day-use area of Ortonville Recreation Area, the second state park unit reached on this ride.

Ortonville is a 5,000-acre park that includes 19 lakes and Pinnacle Point, which at 1,200 feet is one of the highest points in

Southeast Michigan. You actually skirted the north border of it on Hegel Road (remember those state land signs?) but the most developed and used portion of the park is Big Fish Lake. The day-use area, a half mile ride in from Hadley Road, features a large picnic area, bathhouse, pavilion, water and a swimming beach.

Stage Four (12 miles) Return to Hadley Road and turn left (south). In 1.8 miles you'll come to a stop sign and intersection with Oakwood Road. Hadley continues south as a dirt road. You turn left (east) on paved Oakwood, that also has narrow shoulders but light traffic.

Within a mile you pass a riding stable and horse farm and at **Mile 50** of the trip, you enter the one-intersection hamlet of Oakwood. On the corner of Oakwood Road and Baldwin Road is the Oakwood Market for pop, candy, other munchies, even deli sandwiches and fresh pizza by the slice.

Turn right (south) on Baldwin (not to be confused with the Baldwin Road that was followed earlier and ran east to west). As if you hadn't already struggled over enough hills today, the longest one arrives at **Mile 52.5**. You shift gears and pump and then enjoy a free ride down its backside. In another mile, you arrive at the intersection of Baldwin and Seymour Lake Road that you passed in the beginning of the trip. Almost home. All that remains is to turn left (east) on Seymour Lake Road and retrace the first 3.5 miles of the trip to arrive back at Oxford at **Mile 57**.

If you're starving, and who isn't after 57 miles on a bike, you can stop at a soft serve ice cream place on Seymour Lake Road just after entering the Oxford Village limits. Near the corner of Seymour Lake Road (Burdick Road) and M-24 is Mark of Oxford, an excellent bakery that makes bagels, great donuts and breads and gooey pastries. Inside are a few tables and a pot of coffee. Practically next door is Rob's Place, the friendly small town tavern that serves hamburgers and other pub food.

Shorter options: The final stage, the ride from Oxford to

Ortonville Recreation Area, makes for a 24-mile round trip along well paved roads with very light traffic. If you have young children and need something even shorter, consider the park road at Holly Recreation Area. This would be a 6-mile round trip along a road where you could stop often at picnic areas and hiking trails.

Bicycle sales, service

Kinetic Systems, 60 S. Main St., Clarkston; ☎ (810) 625-7000.

Orion Bicycle, 1150 S. Lapeer Rd., Lake Orion; ☎ (810) 693-3333.

Town & Country Cyclery, 880 S. Elm, Lapeer; ☎ (810) 664-1313.

Town & Country Cyclery, 3722 Elizabeth Lake Rd., Waterford; ☎ (810) 681-8600.

Assenmacher Cycling Center, G1272 W. Hill Rd., Grand Blanc ☎ (810) 232-2994.

Repair Stand, 509 N. Leroy, Fenton; ☎ (810) 629-3672.

Area Attractions

Northeast Oakland Historical Museum, Oxford; ☎ (810) 628-0410.

Cooke's Dairy Farm, Ortonville; ☎ (810) 627-3329.

Porter's Cider Mill, Goodrich; ☎ (810) 636-7156.

Area Events And Festivals

July: Fourth of July Jubilee, Lake Orion

August: Oakland County 4-H Fair, Davisburg; Michigan Renaissance Festival, Holly.

September: Michigan Renaissance Festival, Holly.

Travel information

Oxford Area Chamber of Commerce, ☎ (810) 628-0410.

Holly Recreation Area, ☎ (810) 399-9390.

Ortonville Recreation Area, ☎ (810) 627-3828.

Harsens Island

Trip Card

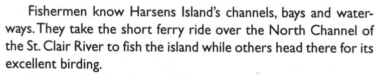

Starting point: Harsens Island
County: St. Clair
Distance: 31.8 miles
Shorter option: 19.4 miles
Terrain: flat
Highlights: wildlife area, St. Clair River, Anchor Bay, island ferry
Suggested riders: beginners

Fishermen know Harsens Island's channels, bays and waterways. They take the short ferry ride over the North Channel of the St. Clair River to fish the island while others head there for its excellent birding.

Harsens Island is located in a unique spot. The 39-mile St. Clair River connects Lakes St. Clair and Huron, and between these two lakes lie several islands. That includes Harsens Island, surrounded by the South, North and Middle Channels of the St. Clair River as well as Big and Little Muscamoot Bays.

For cyclists the island serves up more than 20 miles of primarily paved roads that will lead you on a journey to the island's end. You'll enjoy an area largely untouched by our fast-paced modern times, which lends itself to a rustic "away from it all" feeling that us city dwellers crave. No glitz here...or fudge shops or hordes of tourists either.

There are places to eat here including the Sans Souci Bar

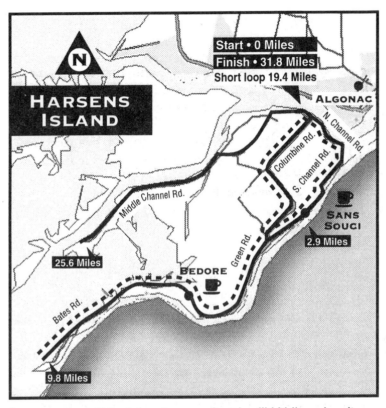

Start • 0 Miles
Finish • 31.8 Miles
Short loop 19.4 Miles

HARSENS ISLAND

ALGONAC

N. Channel Rd.

Columbine Rd.

S. Channel Rd.

Middle Channel Rd.

SANS SOUCI
2.9 Miles

Green Rd.

25.6 Miles

BEDORE

Bates Rd.

9.8 Miles

boasting about "the best pizza on the island". Walkers Landing, a pleasant and soothing spot for refreshments, looks out over the wildlife area and Little Muscamoot Bay.

For the 31.8 mile longer route it's necessary to backtrack a couple of times to see all the scenery the island has to offer. But heck, with scarcely traveled roads and a free afternoon, what else do you have to do but spend time exploring an island less than 30 miles from northern Detroit.

Stage one (9.8 miles) Champion Ferry is located off M-29 in Algonac (follow signs). The ferry costs $4.75, round trip by car; pedestrians and cyclists are free. After disembarking from the ferry, head left on M-154. Where M-154 curves to the right (south), continue straight on North Channel road, a two-lane, tree-lined road.

The North Channel of the St. Clair River is on one side of the road, cottages on the other. Turn right (south) on Orchid Road at **Mile 1** where there's a canopy of trees before the road curves and becomes South Channel Road. This road is lined with more trees and docks extending out on the water. The road makes a couple of sharp curves to keep following the water. The Sans Souci Bar is reached at **Mile 2.9**. The restaurant serves up square pizza, homemade cooking and a great view of the South Channel. A gift shop and San Souci Antiques are also located near here.

Follow the curve to your left as you merge into M-154 at **Mile 3.8** and skirt the St. Clair Flats Wildlife Area. At **Mile 5.6** there's a parking area and vault toilets near a popular fishing spot, and in a mile you pass a second DNR access site. The road is bumpy in spots as you cycle through the wildlife area. At **Mile 8.7** you reach Walkers Landing, a place with a vault toilet and a patio with a picnic table overlooking the water. After the road turns into Bates Road you reach the end of the peninsula at **Mile 9.8**. Here you'll be greeted with a nice view to photograph your cycling companions.

Stage two (9.6 miles) Backtrack the way you came where you'll reach M-154 at **Mile 13.2**. Stay on M-154 as it makes a curve to your left and right (not straight to San Souci). On this section of the road you'll find a lot of birds near a scenic wooded section. You're back to the ferry at **Mile 19.4**.

Stage three (12.4 miles) You could end your tour of Harsens Island at this point but then you can't say you explored the *whole island*. To cycle to the other side of Harsens Island continue west on M-154. Turn left (south) on Golf Course Road where M-154 ends at **Mile 20.2**. This a a two-lane road along the other side of the wildlife area. Near the Middle Channel Party Store, turn left (south) on Middle Channel Road at **Mile 22**, a narrow

The dock at Walker's Landing, a popular watering hole on Harsens Island in Lake St. Clair.

road with gravel shoulders. At **Mile 24.5** you get to ride over a bridge with water on both sides.

The road becomes a bit rough with loose gravel at spots but is still manageable on a road bike. From the end of the road, backtrack the way you came to reach the ferry at **Mile 31.8.** Time to load the bikes on the ferry and find some ice cream, such as at Stroh's Old Fashioned Ice Cream Parlor at 430 Pte. Tremble Road in Algonac.

Shorter option (19.4 miles) Follow Stage One and Stage Two to explore one side of the island.

Bicycle sales, service

MGM Bicycles, 301 Cass, Mt. Clemens; ☎ (810) 463-5381.
Bike World, 35574 23 Mile, New Baltimore; ☎ (810) 725-1150.

Tom Nell Bicycles Ltd., 2528 Elizabeth Lake Road, Pontiac; ☎(810) 682-5456.

Scarlett's Schwinn Cycling & Fitness, 203 N. Perry, Pontiac; ☎(810) 333-7843.

Alpine Cycles, 726 Huron Ave., Port Huron; ☎ (810) 982-9281.

MGM Bicycles, 2408 Griswold, Port Huron; ☎(810) 982-3080.

Big Ralph's Cycling & Fitness, 23531 Nine-Mack Dr., St. Clair Shores; ☎ (810) 772-3258.

MGM Bicycles, 22316 Harper, St. Clair Shores; ☎ (810) 777-0357.

Bill's Bike Sales, 31350 Harper, St. Clair Shores; ☎ (810) 294-3888.

Marine City Sport & Bike, 6752 S. River Road, Marine City; ☎(810) 765-9042.

Area events and festivals

June: Idle Hour Yacht Club Millionaire Party, Algonac.

July: Pickerel Tournament, Street Parade, Fireworks, Riverfront Concerts, Algonac; Walpole Island Pow Wow, Canada.

September: Algonac Art Fair, Algonac; Harsens Island Turkey Shoot, Harsens Island Duck Decoy Show, Harsens Island.

Travel information

Walpole Island Indian Reservation, Canada; ☎ (519) 627-1481.
Greater Algonac Chamber of Commerce; ☎ (810) 794-5511.
Algonac State Park; ☎ (810) 765-5605.
Champion Ferry; ☎ (810) 748-3757.
Walpole Island Ferry, Canada; ☎ (519) 677-5679.

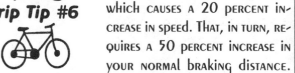

Cycling Trip Tip #6

WET ROADS REDUCE FRICTION which CAUSES A 20 PERCENT INCREASE IN speed. THAT, IN TURN, REQUIRES A 50 PERCENT INCREASE IN YOUR NORMAL braking distance. Also REMEMBER RAIN impairs your visibility.

A cyclist getting ready for the first day of the Pedal Across Lower Michigan (PALM) ride.

 # Michigan Heartland

LakeLands Trail
Irish Hills
Hills & Dales
Lansing River Trail
Ledge Loop
Sleepy Hollow
Chippewa Country

A cyclist makes an adjustment during a break on the LakeLands Rail-Trail in the town of Gregory.

9

LakeLands Trail

Trip Card

Starting point: Stockbridge
Counties: Ingham and Livingston
Distance: 21 miles one-way
Shorter option: 11 miles round trip
Terrain: Flat
Highlights: Rail-trail, small towns of Stockbridge and Gregory, Huron River
Suggested Riders: Beginners

I'm tooling along on my bike, enjoying the surrounding wetlands when I approach a pothole pond and eight mallards explode from the surface a few yards in front of me. This is 10 minutes after I've watched a whitetail deer cross the trail from a corn field and disappear into a tract of woods.

What is more amazing, the abundance of wildlife I'm encountering in Southeast Michigan or the fact that I've already covered 10 miles on this trail but still have another 10 miles to go? A 20-mile trail in the state's most urbanized corner? Don't be surprised. Someday LakeLands Trail State Park will be a 38-mile corridor stretching across four counties from Jackson to Wixom.

Abandoned by the railroad in 1978, LakeLands Trail was established as the state's third linear state park in 1989 when the rail corridor was transferred from the Department of Transportation to the Parks Division of the Department of Natural Resources.

It is split between two sections. The West Unit is a 29-mile

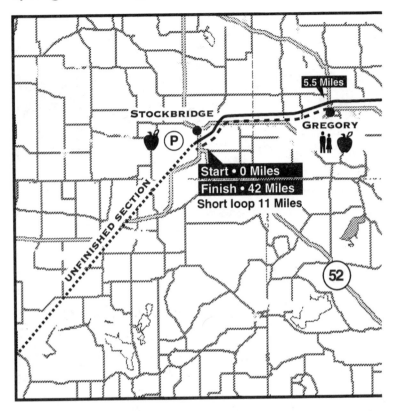

route that begins 5.5 miles north of Jackson and ends at Hamburg while the East Unit is a nine-mile stretch from South Lyon to Wixom in Oakland County.

On National Trails Day in 1994, a 13-mile stretch from Stockbridge to Pinckney was officially opened and the following year the seven-mile extension to Hamburg was added. When the nine-mile section from Stockbridge to Jackson County will be finished is anybody's guess as landowners' disputes about trespassing, typical of any rail-trail project, have to be resolved first.

This tour is the 20-mile, one-way ride from Stockbridge in Ingham County to Hamburg in Livingston County. Like most other rail-trails, LakeLands has been graded, prepared with crushed slag, signposted and connected with designated staging areas. The sur-

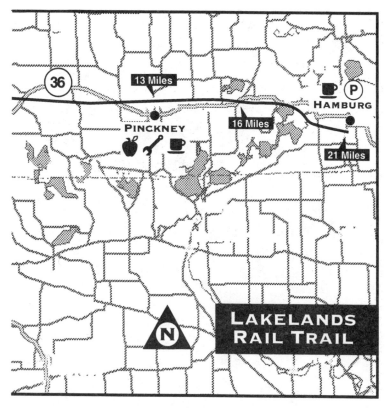

face is ideal for hybrid and mountain bikes but can also be managed with road bicycles without expending too much energy.

Trail Fees: A special trail pass is needed to use the LakeLands Trail. Individual passes are $2 a day and $10 a year while family passes are $5 a day and $25 a year. They can be purchased at the Pinckney Recreation Area headquarters, as well as True Rider Shop and Village Cyclery in Pinckney. Call the state park office at (313) 426-4913 to find out who is selling the passes in Stockbridge.

Stage one (13 Miles) To reach Stockbridge from I-94, depart at exit 159 between Ann Arbor and Jackson and head north on M-52 through Chelsea. Within 15 miles the state road merges with M-106, passes the staging area for the LakeLands Trail and

The LakeLands State Park, administered by the Department of Natural Resources, includes the historic depot in Pinckney.

then enters downtown Stockbridge. This is a picturesque community anchored in the center by a large village green park and its
historic town hall, designed by Elijah E. Myers, the architect who
was also responsible for the state capitol building. Hungry before
or after the ride? Try the German Restaurant and Sausage House
just a block north of the town square area.

The staging area in Stockbridge for the LakeLands Trail is a
Park & Ride lot off of M-106 on the south side of town. The trail
skirts the back side of Stockbridge, past red barns and a scenic
little creek to again arrive at M-106 within a mile and cross the
paved road.

On the other side you leave Stockbridge behind and enter the
country on a trail that is "railroad straight" and very level. The
scenery alternates between farm fields and patches of marsh, small
ponds, stands of hardwoods and ducks on the water. In the woods,
you'll often see deer tracks across the trail.

At **Mile 3.5** you cross Dutton Road. The scenery of alternat-
ing farm fields with small marshes and stands of trees continues
until you cross Van Syckle Road and enter the town of Gregory at
Mile 5.5 from Stockbridge. This is another quaint hamlet where
to the right along Greogry Road (also M-36) is Howlett Hardware, an old-fashioned, hammer-and-nail type of shop that was
established in 1885. Also nearby is a street sign pointing the way
to "Hell"...Michigan that is. Right along the trail is a towering grain
mill that now houses the Old Mill Restaurant which features pizza,
ice cream cones and tables outside. There is also a convenience
store located next door.

In a little more than a mile after departing Gregory you cross
Arnold Road, a dirt country road. Then the scenery changes when
you arrive at M-36 at **Mile 8.2**, only the third time since leaving
Stockbridge that you encounter a paved road. Continuing east
more residential homes pop into view on the north side of the
trail while on the south side is a fenced-in biological field study
area that is maintained by the University of Michigan.

At **Mile 10.5**, you cross Kelly Road, a gravel road, and on the other side enter the Pinckney Recreation Area, the state park which administers the LakeLands Trail. The scenery improves immensely here as the trail becomes a route through open woods and marshland where four times you cross small bridges over Honey Creek. Eventually you cross Clear Lake Road, a gravel road, and M-36 almost simultaneously and enter the town of Pinckney. At **Mile 13** you arrive at the old red train depot on the north side of Pinckney, an official staging area for the LakeLands Trail.

To reach the heart of Pinckney, head south on Pearl Street and then west (right) on M-36. There are several restaurants here, including Aunt Betty's which promises homecooking and Towne Square for pizza and subs. The Village Cyclery bike shop is also located on M-36 (see Tour 3 for a connecting route through Pinckney).

Stage two (8 Miles) Departing east, you pedal through the back side of Pinckney, merging onto a private road briefly just before departing the outskirts of the town. For the next 2.5 miles you pass the backyards of homes and businesses that are now proliferating along M-36. The trail is never that far from the state highway and usually you can see and hear the traffic along it.

The exception is where the trail crosses a high railroad trestle over Hay Creek, reached a mile after you cross Farley Road. Standing on the trestle, you're back in the country, looking at the clear stream gurgling below you or a hilltop cemetery nearby. Just beyond Hay Creek you cross Chambers Road and then at **Mile 16** come to busy M-36. Just to the north (left) on the way to the hamlet of Pettysville is a restaurant and a convenience store.

Carefully cross M-36 and resume riding on the rail-trail which immediately passes behind the Hamburg Township Police and Fire Station. You're now on the south side of M-36 and in 1.3 miles the existing railroad begins to parallel the rail-trail. The two remain within sight of each other all the way to Hamburg.

At **Mile 18** you cross Kress Road and then emerge at Zukey Lake to briefly skirt its north shore and pass a string of lakeside homes. From the lake the next mile is predominantly woods where you cross the Huron River over a long railroad trestle. This is another scenic spot to pause as the river is a wide waterway with usually a canoe or two on it during the summer.

From the woods you emerge at Merrill Road at **Mile 19.2**, Just to the right (south) is Hamburg Township Park (restrooms, picnic tables). Just to the north, at the corner of M-36, is a soft serve ice cream shop. The final leg to Hamburg is through a marshy area where you cross O'Connor Drain and then enter this small hamlet.

Across Hamburg Drive is **Mile 21** and the east end staging area for the LakeLands Trail. Head north on Hamburg Drive to reach the town where you'll find a grocery store, a beer-and-hamburger pub and the classic Hamburg Hardware Store. Want to keep cycling? Tour 3 also passes through Hamburg.

Future Development: The final portion of the LakeLands Trail is a nine-mile leg from Stockbridge to the west end staging area at Hawkins Road near the Jackson State Prison Farm and 5.5 miles northeast of Jackson. Plans also call for the development of a trail rest area in the town of Munith, roughly halfway along this stretch.

Presently land ownership disputes have prevented the trail from being developed, though mountain bikers are already riding portions of it. The trail end across from the Stockbridge staging area is currently blocked off but you can bypass the disputed section by heading north on M-52 and then west on Morton Road for a mile. Turn left (south) on Moechel Road and follow it for more than 2 miles to pick up the rail trail on the west side. From here it is a 3-mile ride to Munith.

Shorter option (11 Miles) For a shorter trip where you need to backtrack to your car, try Stockbridge to Gregory, a round trip of 11 miles. Both towns are delightful and in between is scenic countryside.

Bicycle sales, service

Village Cyclery, 109 E. Main St., Pinckney; ☎ (313) 878-0117.

Area Attractions

Hell Creek Horse Ranch, ☎ (313) 878-3632.

Area Events And Festivals

June: Art in the Park, Pinckney; Howell Bike For Burns.

Travel Information

Pinckney Recreation Area, ☎ (313) 426-4913.

Livingston County Visitors Bureau, ☎ (517) 548-1795 or (800) 686-8474.

Cycling Trip Tip #7

What size of frame should you use? Stand over the bike in your riding shoes and measure the clearance between your crotch and the cross tube. There should be one to two inches for a road bike. But for a mountain bike it's better to have a smaller frame that provides two to three inches of clearance. This will allow you to quickly dismount in case the trail or slope is too challenging for your skill level.

10

Irish Hills

Trip Card

Starting point: Brooklyn
Counties: Lenawee, Jackson
Distance: 42.5 miles
Shorter option: 22 miles
Terrain: rolling hills
Highlights: Brooklyn, Devil's Lake,
W.J. Hayes State Park
Suggested riders: intermediate to advanced

Because the elevations of land resembled their own Ireland, early Irish settlers dubbed their new Michigan settlement the "Irish Hills". In the late 1800's, there were moonlight steamboat cruises for train loads of visitors.

The area has been rediscovered in recent years to continue its tradition as a tourist mecca. Today the Irish Hills, within an hour's drive of Detroit, Toledo, Lansing and Coldwater, beckons travelers with its rolling hills, 52 sparkling lakes, resorts, cottages and an array of attractions such as fudge shops, water slides, bumper boats, miniature golf, an historic tavern, antiques, gardens, bed-and-breakfasts and the Michigan International Speedway.

So what about cycling? Except for the four race weekends at the Michigan International Speedway, the area is delightful for cycling. The rolling hills, roadways with wide paved shoulders and narrow roads winding around Devil's and Wamplers lakes make this a fun ride with a variety of scenery. Members of the Downriver Cycling Club, who supplied this route, use it as a conditioning ride. You get to check out the towns of Brooklyn and Onsted, travel by a state park and wind your way around serene lakes.

The route begins in Brooklyn, the hub of the Irish Hills, and is reached by departing I-94 in Jackson at exit 142 and heading south on US-127. Within 5 miles you exit onto M-50 and follow it into Brooklyn. A grassy meridian slices the road through the downtown area, where you'll find many food choices, shops and an antique mall to keep the non-cyclists in your group busy.

Stage one (9.6 miles) You'll notice plenty of food establishments in Brooklyn including a 1950's style McDonalds and a bakery. Head north on Brooklyn Road out of the business district and into a residential section. Within a quarter mile turn right (east) at the sign pointing to Case Road, which immediately veers left at the fork. You make your way up the first of many hills on this route here and then eventually go downhill past Wolf Lake Road before curving uphill to your right at **Mile 1.6**.

You pass Antcliff Road at **Mile 2.4**. Follow the curve to your right onto Horning Road to continue cycling east. Horning Road, with narrow paved shoulders, twists and curves through a tunnel of trees at **Mile 3**. Looking straight ahead you'll see rolling hills where you can pick up the speed. Turn right onto Hardcastle Road at **Mile 4.7**. This two-lane road begins uphill through some exceptionally beautiful countryside. There's a mixture of homes and cornfields before the road goes downhill past a small waterway within two miles.

At **Mile 7**, turn left (east) onto Wamplers Lake Road (also labeled M-124) where there's a gas station and fresh produce for sale. The road, with wide gravel shoulders, follows Wamplers Lake, although you're in the vicinity of two others - Mud Lake and Round Lake. There's a nice view of Wamplers Lake, a recreational lake, at **Mile 8** before you pass Lakeshore Drive and some small cottages.

The road curves around the lake to the south with a few hills along the way. At **Mile 9.3** is the W.J. Hayes State Park, a park split up the middle by Wamplers Lake Road. The campground entrance to the state park is reached in another third of a mile.

W.J. Hayes State Park, a 654-acre unit, touches the corners of Jackson, Lenawee and Washtenaw counties. Gentle rolling hills are featured in the southern half of the park while the northern portion is the shoreline of Wamplers and Round lakes. The 210-

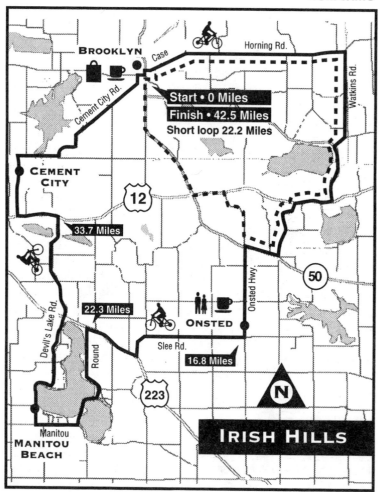

BROOKLYN

Case

Horning Rd.

Watkins Rd.

Start • 0 Miles
Finish • 42.5 Miles
Short loop 22.2 Miles

Cement City Rd.

CEMENT CITY

12

33.7 Miles

Devil's Lake Rd.

22.3 Miles

ONSTED

Onsted Hwy.

50

Slee Rd.

16.8 Miles

Round

223

N

IRISH HILLS

Manitou
MANITOU BEACH

site campground, on the south and west sides of Round Lake, features modern and semi-modern sites including wooded and semi-open sites. There is a 2-mile trail that begins at the back of the campground. Also within the state park is a day-use area with restrooms, drinking water, picnic tables and shelters. There is no entry fee for cyclists riding into a state park.

Stage two (15.2 miles) Continue south on Wamplers Lake Road, passing the Wamplers Lake public access on the right at **Mile 9.7**. You'll go up and down a few more hills before reaching US-12 at **Mile 10**.

After turning right onto US-12 you'll notice a Dairy Bar on your left followed by a fiberglass wicker factory outlet, a family arcade and water slide within a half mile. Many more Irish Hills attractions are also located on US-12 such as Family Fun Center - Bear's Lair, Port-to-Port Adventure Golf, Stagecoach Stop USA, Mystery Hill, Prehistoric Forest dinosaur park and the Walker Tavern Historic Complex. Near **Mile 11** is Kelly's on the Hill, a restaurant with homemade pizza. This road can be busy at times but is manageable because of wide paved shoulders. Turn left (south) onto Springville Highway where a fun hill is enjoyed through a lush section of trees and wildflowers. This lightly traveled road is fairly narrow with no shoulders.

Springville Highway twists and turns past by some homes and lots of views of water as you'll be close to Kellys, Killarney and Cambridge lakes. This area is one of the highlights of the route. Before you turn right (west) onto M-50 at **Mile 13**, you'll travel through a wooded area sprinkled with wildflowers in early summer. M-50 can be busy, although there are wide gravel shoulders. At **Mile 14.2**, turn left (south) onto Onsted Highway. There are plenty of hills on Onsted Highway which heads due south.

You will pass the Country Kids Frosty Boy as you enter the town of Onsted at **Mile 16**. There's a country market on your right followed by a couple of hometown restaurants in the next half mile. The road turns into Main Street before you turn right onto Slee Road at **Mile 16.8** by the high school. The route passes a cemetery, corn and - you guessed it - more hills including a nice downhill at **Mile 19.3** before you make a sharp curve to your left.

At **Mile 20.6**, turn right (northwest) onto US-223, a road you'll follow for less than 2 miles. Turn left (south) onto Round Lake Highway at **Mile 22.3**. There's an arched entrance to the lake at Clearwater Beach in this area. The road is a bit bumpy but has nice views of Devil's Lake. The road narrows a bit and makes a sharp curve to your left at **Mile 23.8**. Use caution here as you wind your way through this scenic resort area.

Devil's and Round lakes were first inhabited by Indians, and legend has it that a princess, who went swimming one day at the north end of Devil's Lake, was never seen again. The Indians de-

Popular Devil's Lake in the Irish Hills area of Michigan's Heartland.

cided that was a sign that the devil must reside there. A rocky area on the east shore was known as "Devil's Chair", and a very deep spot in Echo Cove as "Devil's Hole."

The road is narrow like an alley in parts as you wind around the lake. Some of the docks along this stretch are close enough to touch. Though Round Lake highway is narrow with no shoulders, it's definitely an enjoyable ride and includes a one-lane bridge at **Mile 24.8.** The Devil's Lake area makes a nice spot to park the bikes by the water and take a break.

Stage three (17.7 miles) After you cross the one-lane bridge turn right (west) onto Manitou Road by the Sterling Food Store at **Mile 25.6.** This two-lane road with no shoulders can be a bit busy. You'll pass a supermarket, post office and township park before making a right (north) onto Devil's Lake Highway at **Mile**

26.8. The road twists and curves through another resort area and then passes a DNR access site that is equipped with vault toilets. Devil's Lake Campground is on the left at **Mile 30.4** just before you reach a busy intersection at US-223.

Beyond US-223, Devil's Lake Road continues north through farmland and over more hills. The road narrows a bit as you make your way uphill at **Mile 32.2**, then hit a stretch that has been recently resurfaced. Before you make a left (west) onto US-12 at **Mile 33.7**, you'll cycle past a canal.

You are now back on the wide, paved shoulders of US-12, which again can be busy road. You'll pass Irish Hills Resort Campground before turning right (north) onto Cement City Highway at **Mile 35**. Cement City is reached within 1.5 miles but there's not a whole lot to this "city" except some residences, a boat launch and a barn. At the Cement City Baptist Church turn right (east) just before Cement City Highway enters Jackson County and becomes Cary Road. This puts you on Cement City Road, which makes a sharp curve to the left (north) and then to the right (east) at **Mile 38.8**.

This is a nice stretch of road as it's lightly traveled in open country. Cement City Road heads northeast to Brooklyn by making a sharp curve to the right at Kelley Road at **Mile 39.7**. You're back in Brooklyn within a mile. Once in the village Cement City Road becomes King Street. Turn right (east) onto Marshall Street and then right (south) on Brooklyn Road to reach the town's business district at **Mile 42.5**. Time to rest, eat some fudge and maybe try the arcade or miniature golf.

Shorter option (22 miles) To shorten the route follow Stage One to the W.J. Hayes State Park and the beginning of State Two. Instead of taking a left (south) onto Onsted Highway, turn right (north). From Onsted Highway turn left (west) onto US-12, right (north) onto US 50 and right (north) on Brooklyn Road.

Special note: It is imperative that you skip bicycling in the Irish Hills area during the four major race weekends at the Michigan International Speedway (MIS) in June, July, August and September. For exact dates call the MIS office at (800) 354-1010.

Bicycle sales, service

Barber's Bike Shop, 929 Lansing, Jackson; ☎ (517) 782-2789.

Toy House, 400 N. Mechanic, Jackson; ☎ (517) 787-4500.

On Two Wheels, 550 Laurence, Jackson; ☎ (517) 789-6077.

Pedal and Tour, 3322 Francis, Jackson; ☎ (517) 789-6362.

Adrian Locksmith & Cyclery, 611 N. Main St., Adrian; ☎ (517) 263-1415.

Smith Cyclery, 113 W. Maumee, Adrian; ☎ (517) 265-8555.

The Peak, 1416 S. Main St., Adrian; ☎ (517)263-8902.

Area attractions

Stagecoach Stop USA, Onsted; ☎ (517) 467-2300.

Michigan International Speedway, Brooklyn; ☎ (800) 354-1010.

Family Fun Center - Bear's Lair, Tipton; ☎ (517) 431-2217.

Port-to-Port Adventure Golf, Tipton; ☎ (517) 431-2262.

Hidden Lake Gardens, Tipton; ☎ (517) 431-2060.

Walker Tavern, Irish Hills; ☎ (517) 467-4414.

Pinetree Centre Antique Mall, Brooklyn; ☎ (517) 592-3808.

Area events and festivals

June: Children's Day I at Walker Tavern; Outdoor Party and Chicken Barbeque, Stagecoach USA; Brooklyn Artists' Arts & Crafts Show; Stock Car Race at MIS, Brooklyn.

July: Bluegrass Festival, Brooklyn; Civil War Reenactment, 19th Century Days, at Walker Tavern Historic Complex; Marlboro 500 at MIS, Brooklyn.

August: Jackson & Lenawee County Fair; Brooklyn Artists' Arts & Craft Show, Brooklyn; Detroit Gasket 200, Michigan International Speedway, Brooklyn; Children's Day II at Walker Tavern; Bluegrass Jamboree at Stagecoach Stop USA.

September: GM Teamwork 300 at MIS, Brooklyn; Half Way to St. Pat's Day Golf Tournament, Brooklyn-Irish Hills.

October: Arts & Crafts Show, Brooklyn.

Travel information

Brooklyn-Irish Hills Chamber of Commerce; ☎ (517) 592-8907.

W.J. Hayes State Park; ☎ (517) 467-7401.

The Grosvenor House Museum in Jonesville is a 19th century manison that was designed by the same architect who designed the state capitol in Lansing.

11

Hills & Dales

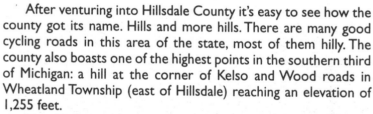

Trip Card
Starting point: Litchfield
County: Hillsdale
Distance: 41.2 miles
Shorter option: 8 miles round trip
Terrain: rolling hills
Highlights: Litchfield, Jonesville, Hillsdale, small lakes
Suggested riders: advanced

After venturing into Hillsdale County it's easy to see how the county got its name. Hills and more hills. There are many good cycling roads in this area of the state, most of them hilly. The county also boasts one of the highest points in the southern third of Michigan: a hill at the corner of Kelso and Wood roads in Wheatland Township (east of Hillsdale) reaching an elevation of 1,255 feet.

This 40 plus-mile route lets cyclists, looking for a conditioning route, sample the area and savor the peaceful atmosphere of small towns and scenic country roads. It roams through the towns of Litchfield, Jonesville and Hillsdale. These communities are tucked away between urban areas, giving cyclists an opportunity to discover and explore a worthwhile county.

Litchfield, a picturesque village of just over 1,300 residents and your starting point for this route, has a downtown area in the shape of a semi-circle, a town square of sorts. It's another one of Michigan's quintessential small towns with a homey, Americana appeal. Good old-fashioned gatherings take place in Litchfield, like the city-wide yard sales and the Seed Corn Fest in June, the Threshers Show in July and Sweet Corn Days in September. How's that for rural flavor?

To add to the small town feel, Litchfield boasts a large collection of antique tools from the turn of the century. The Litchfield Community Hand Tool Collection, with more than 100 tools, is located in the Litchfield Town Hall, near the center of town. To reach Litchfield from the east side of the state, depart I-94 at exit 136 (just west of Jackson) and head southwest on M-60. In the town of Homer, head south on M-99 to reach Litchfield in 8 miles.

This route also takes you to Hillsdale, the county seat. With plenty of food choices, this town of 8,000 is a good place to stop 31 miles into the route. You can see Hillsdale's Victorian tradition in the town courthouse and many other structures. The city's historic area features a renovated shopping district, Victorian street lights and specialty shops. You'll cycle past Hillsdale College "on the hill" where you'll notice the college's central hall clock tower just above the trees.

Jonesville, the second oldest community in Hillsdale County, hosts plenty of events including the Frontier Days Canoe Race. The town has many historic, private homes. One of the more famous structures, the Grosvenor House Museum, was constructed in 1874 and is now listed on the National Register of Historic Places. The structure was built for Ebenezer Grosvenor, a Jonesville banker and former state treasurer, who had a major role in the construction of our state captiol.

A little history, a lot of hills and pleasant small towns add up to an enjoyable route. Plan your visit to Hillsdale County, mentally prepare yourself for some hills and enjoy!

Stage one (12.5 miles) There's parking around the business district of Litchfield, including public parking across from Joe's Bar & Grill near the heart of Litchfield on M-99. From the downtown area (near Field's Creme Supreme, for ice cream, and the Litchfield Township Office) cycle to the left (east) on St. Joe Street which will turn into Litchfield Road. This two-lane, lightly traveled road is a mixture of residential sections, open country and shaded areas. After the first of many hills on this route, you'll find yourself out of town among the corn and wildflowers.

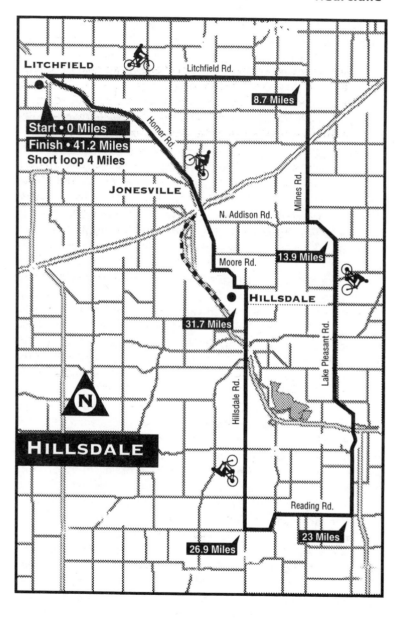

LITCHFIELD

Litchfield Rd.

8.7 Miles

Homer Rd.

Start • 0 Miles
Finish • 41.2 Miles
Short loop 4 Miles

JONESVILLE

Milnes Rd.

N. Addison Rd.

Moore Rd.

13.9 Miles

31.7 Miles

HILLSDALE

Lake Pleasant Rd.

Hillsdale Rd.

N

HILLSDALE

Reading Rd.

26.9 Miles

23 Miles

Beginning at **Mile 4.7** there's a little bit of loose stone on the road, still manageable on your 12-speed. You'll enjoy a pretty, tree-lined section with lots of big old hardwoods including a weeping willow tree. Past the intersection of Concord and Litchfield, you'll cycle through a residential section and past Cobb Lake, a small waterway, at **Mile 6.5**.

No more loose stone after you make a right (south) onto Milnes Road at **Mile 8.7**. This two-lane, paved country road has plenty of trees and pleasant farms. After you pass Hastings Lake Road within a mile, there's more rolling hills before you come to a blinking four-way stop at the intersection of US-12 and Milnes Road. *Careful: US-12, (also called Chicago Road) can be busy.* At **Mile 12.5** the road climbs a hill with cornfields on both sides. This may be a good time to stop, catch your breath and drink from your water bottle to prepare for more hills and a long second stage.

Stage two (19.4 miles) Turn left (east) onto North Adams Road to reach Lake Pleasant Road. There's a fruit stand and greenhouse to your right and wildflowers and farmland elsewhere. The road curves to the right beginning at **Mile 12.8** before making a sharp curve to your left; an uphill section begins within a mile. Turn right onto Lake Pleasant Road at **Mile 13.9**, a hilly, two-lane road with gravel shoulders. You'll enjoy careening downhill before you pass Lake Bel-Air.

Make a quick left (east) onto Peterson Road and then a right back onto Lake Pleasant Road at **Mile 19**. At the yield sign, veer to the right to reach a fun section of small rolling hills and sloping green lawns through a residential section. Follow the road as it makes a couple of sharp curves before crossing M-99 at **Mile 20.2**, and then in roughly a half mile make a hard left (east) to stay on Lake Pleasant Road.

There are lush cornfields before you make a right (west) onto Reading Road by a scenic cemetery at **Mile 23**. More trees, corn and - you guessed it - more rolling hills. Within a mile you will pass Doty Road and climb even more hills (how's this for a conditioning ride?). The road goes downhill and makes a sharp curve to your left before reaching Steamburg Road at **Mile 26**.

In a mile turn right (north) onto Hillsdale Road, a sometimes busy, two-lane road with gravel shoulders. Hillsdale Road is a straight, north-south road, with rolling hills, scenic farms and wild-flowers gracing the road throughout much of the summer. Natu-rally, you'll make your way uphill before you reach the city limits of Hillsdale at *Mile 31.7*. Hillsdale Road is called Howell Road in town and you'll cycle by some historic homes to reach an exten-sive downtown area. Time to lock'em up, stroll through town and try out one of the restaurants. Most of Hillsdale's restaurants are located on Howell Road including a local favorite, Mancino's Pizza.

Stage three (8.3 miles) From downtown Hillsdale head north on Hillsdale Road. You'll pass Hillsdale College on your left at *Mile 32.5*. The liberal arts college, founded in 1844, is an inde-pendent residential college of approximately 1,000 students. On Hillsdale Street near the college are many historic homes includ-ing the Delta Sigma Phi fraternity house at 139 Hillsdale St., built in the early 1850's, and the Chandler-Cook house at 172 Hillsdale St., a Greek Revival home built in 1853.

After you make a left (west) onto Moore Road at *Mile 33.7*, you'll climb a few hills, encounter some sharp curves and reach a railroad crossing in the next two miles. Turn right (north) onto Homer Road (not marked). Continue straight into Jonesville where the road turns into Maumee Street. In town, the historic Jonesville Village Hall is on your left, along with a bakery. At 211 Maumee Street you'll find the Grosvenor House Museum, open from 2-5 p.m. on weekends throughout the summer. Also stop at the Jonesville Village Hall right on US-12, which houses a Deal Motors Company car, one of only two known to exist (the other is part of a private collection in Nevada). The Jonesville company was fa-mous for its car warranty: no matter where the car broke down, a Deal Motors mechanic would come out to fix it. If we only had such car warranties today!

Continue north on Homer Road, also called M-99; it's now 7 miles back to Litchfield. This road can be busy but there are nicely paved shoulders on both sides. At *Mile 38.5*, there's an expansive barn complex. There is a park with a picnic area within a mile and the Litchfield city limits are reached at *Mile 40.2*. A mile later you will be back at the starting point of the route. Congratula-tions! You've completed one of the most strenuous routes mapped out in this book.

Note: To lengthen this route, or as an interesting side trip, check out the town of Allen, located a little more than 5 miles south of Litchfield on M-49. Allen is the unofficial antique capital of Michigan. A person could browse for hours at the dozen or so antique shops along a stretch of US-12. The development sprang up in the early 1970's when several antique shops opened at the same time on US-12.

Shorter option (8 miles round trip) Between Jonesville and Hillsdale, running parallel to M-99, there is a separate 4-mile bicycle path. In Hillsdale the path is located less than a mile north of the downtown area on M-99, on the left hand side of the road just past a plaza of small shops and a Subway Restaurant. Future plans call for the path to extend on through Hillsdale and out to Sandy Beach. The path in Jonesville is located near Bud's Market on the east side of the road.

Bicycle sales, service
Adrian Locksmith & Cyclery, 611 N. Main, Adrian; ☎ (517) 263-1415.

Smith Cyclery, 113 W. Maumee, Adrian; ☎ (517) 265-8555.

The Peak, 1416 S. Main St., Adrian; ☎ (517) 263-8902.

Area attractions
Slayton Arboretum, Hillsdale College, Hillsdale.

Grosvenor House Museum, Jonesville; ☎ (517) 849-9596.

Will Carleton Pourhouse, Hillsdale; ☎ (517) 439-4341.

Courthouse Square, Hillsdale; ☎ (517) 439-4341.

Area events, festivals
May: Riverfest, Jonesville; Allen Antique Market.

June: Seed Corn Days, Litchfield; Hillsdale Car Show.

July: Allen Antique & Collectibles Market, Allen; 4th of July Celebration, Threshers Show, Hillsdale.

August: Sidewalk Days, Farm Festival, Boat Races, Hillsdale.

September: Allen Antique & Collectibles Market, Allen; Sweet Corn Days, Litchfield; Hillsdale County Fair, Hillsdale.

October: Octoberfest, Halloween Parade, Jonesville.

Travel information
Hillsdale County Chamber of Commerce; ☎ (517) 439-4341.

Lansing River Trail

Trip Card

Starting Point: Lansing
County: Ingham
Distance: 20 miles
Shorter Option: 9.4 miles
Terrain: primarily flat
Highlights: Grand River, Red Cedar River, Potter Park Zoo, museums, Michigan State University
Suggested riders: beginners and families

Families looking for a route with few hills, lots of attractions and pleasant scenery should consider Lansing's River Trail. Combined with a circular tour of Michigan State University's campus, this 20-mile ride is a fun jaunt for riders of every ability.

The River Trail has been around since the mid-70s and it's often crowded with in-line skaters, joggers, hikers and cyclists. Because of this heavy use it's not a trail for racing; rather it's better suited for taking the kids on a leisurely tour with plenty of attractions to stop at along the way. Eventually the trail will connect with MSU, but for now Kalamazoo Street with its paved shoulders is the connecter to the large, scenic campus. The trail is six miles from end to end.

River Trail connects several parks including Riverfront Park, home of Lansing's major festivals, and many historic sites. The trail will give cyclists a sampling of natural beauty along the Grand and Red Cedar rivers as well as a journey through the state capital, our "nerve center" of Michigan.

Ideally situated in Lansing, and close to East Lansing, the River Trail is a fun route to combine with other activities. You can combine cycling and a Big 10 football game, a concert, a tour of the State Capitol, one of the many Lansing museums or a stroll along Grand River Avenue in East Lansing to browse through shops and bookstores.

Stage one (6 miles) There are many places you can park along the trail including the Potter Park Zoo and the Impression Five Museum located near downtown. There's also Dietrich Park at the north edge of the trail by the Turner/Dodge House. At the south end of the trail, we parked in a small lot off Kalamazoo Street near Sparty's Night Club. This is a convenient spot because from here it's easy to add mileage by continuing on to Michigan State University.

The trail winds south along the Red Cedar River. Within a mile, you come to the second of two wooden bridges. At **Mile 2**, you reach the first of many attractions on the trail, the Potter Park Zoo. The zoo features 120 animal species including big cats from Africa and Asia and primates from Madagascar and the Far East. There's an outdoor penguin exhibit and camel rides for those brave enough. Potter Park Zoo also includes scenic picnic areas, canoe rentals, pavilions and restrooms.

For the next 1.5 miles you cycle along the Red Cedar River before its confluence with the Grand River, the spot where the trail swings north. As you make your way toward downtown Lansing you'll come across the first of several attractions within a half mile: the R.E. Olds Transportation Museum, a collection of cars and memorabilia, courtesy of one of Lansing's most famous citizens - R.E. Olds. Children will especially enjoy the Planet Walk that begins just north of the museum. This scale model of our solar system begins with a sun that's 20 inches in diameter, located just outside the Impression Five Museum, and ends at the Potter Park Zoo. Along the River Trail there are plaques for each

planet giving astronomical information.

At the Impressions Five Museum, children learn through "hands on" exhibits about the wonders of science. Good Housekeeping Magazine designated the museum as one of the top ten national science museums. After the museum, the trail wanders within view of the Lansing Center (a convention center), the historic Wentworth and Kerns hotels, the Board of Water and Light and then the Lansing Community College.

A cyclist pauses on the Lansing River Trail, a popular six-mile route through the state capital that passes a variety of attractions.

Before you rejoin the trail after crossing busy Saginaw Street you will cycle through Riverfront Park where Lansing's major festivals take place. Within a quarter mile north of the park you'll see the William A. Brenke River Sculpture and Fish Ladder, located at the North Lansing Dam on Grand River Avenue. It's the place to go to see spawning salmon and steelhead fight their way upstream in August and September.

At the northern tip of the trail you'll find the Turner/Dodge House, built in the early 1850's by James Turner, one of the earliest settlers in the Lansing area. The house is being restored to reflect life in the late 1800's.

Stage two (6 miles) Backtrack on the trail the way you came to reach the parking area on Kalamazoo Street.

Stage three (8 miles) Turn right (east) onto Kalamazoo Street, a shaded and winding road with paved shoulders, to reach the Michigan State University campus. Once on the campus you'll pass the University Village Apartments and then the Breslin Center and Jenison Fieldhouse on Kalamazoo Street. There are many ways to enjoy cycling on the MSU campus. The following route was designed by the Tri-County Bicycle Association and is a 5-mile circular loop including a stop at an ice cream store on Farm Lane. Huge ice cream cones are served by agriculture students at the facility used as a dairy training center.

From Kalamazoo Street, turn right onto West Circle which merges into East Circle. Turn right onto Physics Road, left onto Auditorium, then left onto Farm Lane, a busy 4-lane road with sidewalks on both sides. Farm Lane will take you to the edge of campus where you want to cycle left onto Service and then left on Bogue Street. Bogue will take you past the Horticultural Dem-

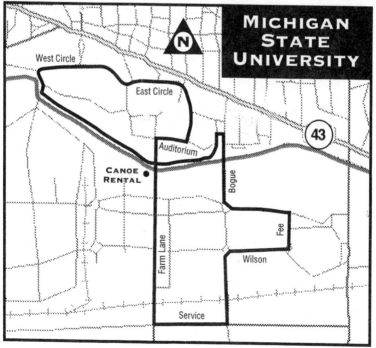

onstration Gardens.

Follow Bogue around the traffic circle and stay on the road to the right, which is Wilson. Turn left onto Fee before making another left onto Shaw. You'll cycle past a variety of dormitories.

Veer north onto another traffic circle, where the road becomes Bogue Street again. Make a short left on Auditorium before heading south on the bike trails along the Red Cedar River, a highlight of the route. You'll pass a canoe rental place and the library before you connect back to Kalamazoo Street and the parking area.

Michigan State University's impressive campus encompasses 2,000 acres. The Red Cedar River meanders through the campus, known for its natural beauty including an expansive variety of trees, shrubs and flowers. The university, founded in 1855, became the nation's first and largest land-grant institution in 1882. With its 40,000 full-time students, MSU impacts the Lansing area in a major way.

Once you've finished cycling, remember it's a college town and there are plenty of pizza places, fast food and numerous other interesting restaurants to choose from. One of my favorite is Bell's Pizza, just off Grand River in East Lansing, for great tuna grinders and Greek salads.

Shorter option (9 miles) Cycling the Lansing River Trail from Kalamazoo Street, near MSU to Saginaw Street and back again makes a nice shorter option that includes most of the attractions along the trail.

Bicycle sales, service

Denny's Schwinn Cycling & Fitness, 1215 E. Grand River, East Lansing; ☎ (517) 351-2000.

Denny's Schwinn Cycling & Fitness, 143 N. Harrison, East Lansing; ☎(517) 332-8655.

Velocipede Peddler, 541 E. Grand River, East Lansing; ☎(517) 351-7240.

Holt Pro Cyclery, 2230 N. Cedar; ☎ (517) 694-6702.

Central Park Bicycles, 1805 Central Park Drive, Okemos; ☎ (517) 349-8880.

Eric's Bicycle Shop, 6070 S. Logan, Lansing; ☎ (517) 882-7003.

Don's Bicycle Service, 1531 Jerome, Lansing; ☎ (517) 372-2122.

Riverfront Cycles, 507 E. Shiawassee, Lansing; ☎ (517) 482-8585.

Denny's Schwinn Cycling & Fitness, 5023 W. Saginaw, Lansing; ☎ (517) 321-6700.

Area events and festivals

May: East Lansing Art Fair.

June: Downtown Lansing Art Fair.

July, August: Ingham County Fair, Mason.

August: Michigan Festival, East Lansing.

September: Riverfest, Lansing.

Area attractions

Impression 5 Science Museum, Lansing; ☎ (517) 485-8115.

Kresge Art Museum, MSU; ☎ (517) 355-7631.

Michigan Library & Historical Center, Lansing; ☎ (517) 373-3559.

Michigan Museum of Surveying, Lansing; ☎ (517) 484-6605.

Michigan State University Museum; ☎ (517) 355-2370.

Michigan Women's Hall of Fame, Lansing; ☎ (517) 484-1880.

The State Capitol, Lansing; ☎ (517) 335-1483.

R.E. Olds Transportation Museum, Lansing; ☎ (517) 372-0422.

Turner Dodge House and Park, Lansing; ☎ (517) 483-4220.

Telephone Pioneer Museum, Lansing; ☎ (517) 372-1400.

Wharton Center for Performing Arts, MSU; ☎ (517) 355-6688 or (800) WHARTON.

Abrams Planetarium, MSU; ☎ (517) 355-4672 or 355-4676.

Travel information

Greater Lansing Visitor's Bureau; ☎ (517) 487-6800.

Capital City River Runners; ☎ (517) 332-2681 or 349-0886.

The famous ledges that border the Grand River near Grand Ledge.

13

Ledge Loop

Trip Card

Starting Point: Grand Ledge
Counties: Eaton, Clinton and Ionia
Distance: 34 miles
Terrain: primarily flat
Highlights: Grand Ledge, one-lane bridge, Grand River ledges
Suggested riders: beginners to intermediate

This well-designed ride was developed by the Tri-County Bicycle Association. It's just the right mix for a few hours of cycling - beautiful countryside, primarily flat roads, the Grand River and small towns strategically placed for breaks.

The ride begins and ends in Grand Ledge, a town of more than 7,000 residents 10 miles west of Lansing. This pleasant community got its name from the Grand River and the sandstone ledges - towering faces of sheer rock that border both sides of the river west of town.

But that's not the only unique feature of the Grand Ledge area; there are seven islands within viewing distance of the downtown business district. The main island on the river is known as Island Park, where most of the town's major events take place. An old iron bridge leads to the narrow island where there are benches, picnic tables, a gazebo and small docks along the shoreline. There's parking for cars at a city lot. River cruises regularly circle the island.

Mention Grand Ledge and many people think of a place to go for birthday and Christmas gifts for that hard-to-buy-for person. The town overflows with antiques, crafts, collectibles, boutiques, hobby shops and other gift shops. Probably the most well-known place in town is Ledge Craft Lane Ltd., at the corner of Bridge and River streets, comprised of 15 booths featuring the works of 150 artists and craftsmen. And on the first Saturday in August, you can enjoy crafts, music, food and riverboat rides (and cycling!) during the Island Art Fair in Grand Ledge.

This ride gives you and your cycling companions plenty of options for shopping, eating or relaxing. Locals recommend hard-packed ice cream at Quality Dairy on Jefferson Street (the main street in town), and Lickity Split Ice Cream, on the Grand River across from the Island. For pizza try Pasquale's Pizza on South Bridge Street or the Log Jam Inn on West Jefferson.

Before or after the ride you'll want to explore the Ledges, one of the most geologically significant areas in lower Michigan. Composed of Eaton Sandstone deposited 250 million years ago, made mostly of quartz grains cemented to iron oxide, the Ledges attract hikers, rock climbers and picnickers from across the Midwest.

Visit Fitzgerald Park, 1.5 miles west of Grand Ledge at 3808 Grand Ledge Highway, to explore the Ledges Trail and check out the caves at the base of the Ledges in the 76-acre park. There are six picnic sites, a fish ladder, and a small nature center here. Fitzgerald Park is a 1.5-mile hike from the Island.

A popular time to visit the Grand Ledge area is during the Color Cruise and Island Festival, held on the second weekend of October. You can view the color by bicycle, riverboat, canoe or horse and buggy. The Princess Laura Riverboat and J&K Steamboat regularly circle the island and the river ledges that gave the city its name.

Stage one (13.8 miles) We parked at Neff Elementary School, near Grand Ledge High School. Neff Elementary is lo-

cated south of the downtown area on Jenne Street. Turn right on Bridge Street and cycle through a residential area. Head north out of Grand Ledge on North Clinton Road, where you'll find open country and farmland. Initially the road is bumpy with partially paved shoulders. *Note: Clinton Road turns into Wright Road (M-100), which can be busy at times.*

At **Mile 4**, turn left onto Grand River Avenue, a wide, two-lane road with no shoulders. Within 2.5 miles you will reach the small town of Eagle, founded in 1834. This scenic section is lined with residences, open areas and picturesque barns. At the corner of Grange Road is the Eagle Party Store and a small grocery store if you're in need of a candy bar or other energy infusions. Past the stores, there's a house on the right with a totem pole, followed by wooded areas and wildflowers growing close to the road. I spotted a cute "McMillan & Husband Antiques" sign on the left. At **Mile 9.7** you enter Ionia County.

Before you reach the town of Portland at **Mile 13.8**, you'll pass a quaint log cabin, cornfields, and a small white church situated among old trees. In Portland, a town of just under 4,000 residents, there are plenty of places for fast food and restrooms.

Stage two (8.8 miles) Caution: Grand River Avenue can be busy in Portland. Turn left onto Bridge Street at **Mile 14**. Shortly you'll want to make another left onto Charlotte Highway. This beautiful stretch of road winds and twists through a mix of open country and shaded, wooded areas. A highlight is a one-lane bridge over the Grand River at **Mile 18**. Stop at the stop sign at the bottom of the hill. But beware: the metal bridge surface can be slippery!

You'll enjoy nice views of the river to your left within a half mile, followed by a long uphill to your left before you reach the Mulliken Village limits at **Mile 21.6**. At this point, the road becomes Mulliken Road as you're in Eaton County now. In this pleasant village, comprised of a few streets backed up by prime farmland, there's a Mulliken Thrifty Way Market at the corner of M-43 and Mulliken Road at **Mile 22.6**.

Stage three (11.7 miles) There's loose stone on parts of Mulliken Road, but for the most part it's still rideable on a road bicycle. From Mulliken Road, turn left at St. Joe Highway at **Mile 24.8**. When we cycled this route in early August, the corn was past knee-high.

For more than 6 miles you can really go for speed on the wide, open St. Joe Highway. At spots you can see the countryside far off into the distance on all four sides.

You'll enjoy lush green fields and a church on the corner of Oneida Road and St. Joe Highway; how peaceful on a quiet, Sunday afternoon! Turn left here onto Oneida Road at **Mile 31** (this road also has some loose stone). In just over a mile, turn right on Saginaw Highway. The road here is flat as you make your way back to Grand Ledge. Turn right onto Grand Ledge Highway (East M-43). The road can be busy and has a combination of gravel and paved shoulders. Turn left onto Jenne Street to cycle back to the school parking lot at Mile **34.3**. Now it's time to go shopping for antiques, take in an art fair or plan your riverboat excursion. If you want more exercise, stretch those legs and hike the ledges at Fitzgerald Park, just west of Grand Ledge on Grand Ledge Highway.

Bicycle sales, service

Denny's Cycling & Fitness, 5023 W. Saginaw, Lansing; ☎ (517) 321-6700.

Discount Peddler, 121 E. Kalamazoo, Lansing; ☎ (517) 372-8088.

Don's Bicycle Services - Bike-A-Van, 1531 Jerome, Lansing; ☎ (517) 372-2122.

Eric's Bicycle Shop, 6070 S. Logan, Lansing; ☎ (517) 882-7003.

Puck & Pedal Pro Shop, 326 Morgan Lane, Lansing; ☎(517) 332-6677.

Riverfront Cycles, 507 E. Shiawassee, Lansing; ☎ (517) 482-8585 or (517) 484-0362.

Area attractions

Ledge Craft Lane; ☎ (517) 627-9843.

Fitzgerald Park; ☎ (517) 627-7351 or (517) 627-5010.

Princess Laura Riverboat (J&K Steamboat); ☎ (517) 627-2154.

Opera House, ☎ (517) 627-2383.

Oak Park (overlooking river and the Ledges), call Vertical Ventures ☎ (517) 485-7681.

Lincoln Brick Park, ☎ (517) 627-7351 or (517) 627-9010.

Area events and festivals

June: International Bowhunter's Clinic, Yankee Doodle Days, Oneida Field Market, Grand Ledge.

August: Island Art Fair, Grand Ledge.
September: Oneida Field Market, Grand Ledge.
October: Color Cruise & Island Festival, Grand Ledge.
Travel information
Grand Ledge Area Chamber of Commerce; ☎ (517) 627-2383.

Cycling Trip Tip #8

CONTEMPLATING A CENTURY RIDE? FOR MOST CYCLIST COVERING A 100 MILES IN A DAY IS QUITE AN ACHIEVEMENT ANY TIME, BUT ESPECIALLY THE FIRST TIME THEY ACCOMPLISH IT. KEEP IN MIND THAT LONG, SINGLE-DAY RIDES REQUIRE ENDURANCE WHICH IN TURN REQUIRES TRAINING. WHEN YOU BEGIN A BIKING SEASON IN THE SPRING, RIDE IN THE LOWER GEARS TO EASE THE STRAIN ON KNEES. PLAN ON AT LEAST ONE LONG RIDE EACH WEEK AND USE THIS BOOK TO PICK OUT NEW ROUTES TO KEEP IT INTERESTING. THEN EACH WEEK STRIVE TO INCREASE THE LENGTH OF THAT RIDE FIVE TO 10 PERCENT. FINALLY, LIKE RUNNERS WHO ENTER MARATHONS, YOU CAN ALSO COUNT ON RIDING THREE TIMES AS LONG AS YOUR AVERAGE TRAINING PERIOD. IF YOU TRAIN FOR TWO HOURS DURING THE WEEK, YOU SHOULDN'T HAVE ANY PROBLEM COVERING A SIX TO EIGHT HOUR TOUR ON THE WEEKEND.

14

Sleepy Hollow

Trip Card

Starting Point: Lake Lansing
Counties: Ingham, Clinton, Shiawassee
Distance: 43.5 miles
Shorter Option: 4 miles
Terrain: mostly flat
Highlights: Lake Lansing, Laingsburg, Sleepy Hollow State Park
Suggested riders: beginners to intermediate

At 2,000 members, the Tri-County Bicycle Association is one of Michigan's largest bike clubs. Cyclists who join the club in the Lansing area, where road bike sales top those of mountain bicycles, receive a booklet of routes with well laid out maps.

Club officials graciously sent me the book of maps so I could sample some of their routes. This route and others (Grand Ledge and River Trail) have been adapted from tours in that booklet.

Lake Lansing South County Park, east of East Lansing, provides a convenient starting point for many routes in the area. The popular, busy park surrounds the triangular-shaped Lake Lansing, a watery oasis in this landlocked area and the only waterway big enough for boating in the Lansing area. The park includes areas for swimming, hiking, picnicking, rowboat and paddle boat rentals, as well as exceptionally nice restrooms, a rarity in many parks. It's a great place to drop off your non-cycling companions while you ride this 43-mile loop. Flat roads, lots of straightaways and countryside views make this an enjoyable and fairly easy route. Laingsburg (population: 1,148), one of Michigan's quintessential small towns and the 2,500-acre Sleepy Hollow State Park also make this a route with just the right mix of diversity.

Lansing and adjacent East Lansing brim with activities and attractions, making this a popular area to combine cycling with Big 10 sports, a tour of our State Capitol or a host of museums. (see River Trail for description of various museums)

Food? Not to worry. Fifteen miles into the route in Laingsburg there's Nick's Pizza in a renovated train depot, as well as another restaurant, a couple of bars and a convenience store in town. After your ride, there are hundreds of choices in East Lansing and Lansing including a smorgasbord of fast food choices.

Stage one (15.1 miles) From the parking lot at Lake Lansing County Park South, turn left (south) onto Marsh Road, a sometimes busy road with sidewalks on either side. At the stop light, cycle left (east) onto Lake Lansing Road, which can be a busy intersection. There are sidewalks on both sides. Lake Lansing Road heads toward the lake, curves to the right and becomes Shaw Street at **Mile 0.7**. This narrow, lightly traveled road follows the lake. You will cross Lake Drive, where you need to be sure to check traffic before you make a left (east) onto Haslett Road, a busy four-lane road with sidewalks on both sides.

Haslett Road goes through Haslett, a town of just over 10,000 residents. After the road makes a sharp curve to your right and you travel through a pleasant residential area, turn left (north) onto Green Road at **Mile 2.5**. Green Road has two lanes, with sidewalks on the right-hand side.

The predominantly flat road goes through a residential area, with lots of trees and big yards to look at. There are a few dips in the road for a rolling hill effect. Turn right (east) onto Barry Road, a two lane road with no shoulders, at **Mile 4.4**. You'll cycle through a nice, level section for a half mile before you reach a downhill that rolls and makes a couple of curves.

Turn left (north) onto Shoeman Road at **Mile 5**. This is a spot in Ingham County that is close to Shiawassee and Clinton counties. The road turns into two-lane Woodbury Road (Welcome to Shiawassee County) before you cycle over a railroad track. Here you'll find a mixture of residential and open land. The fairly flat road makes a couple of curves, travels past a majestic weeping

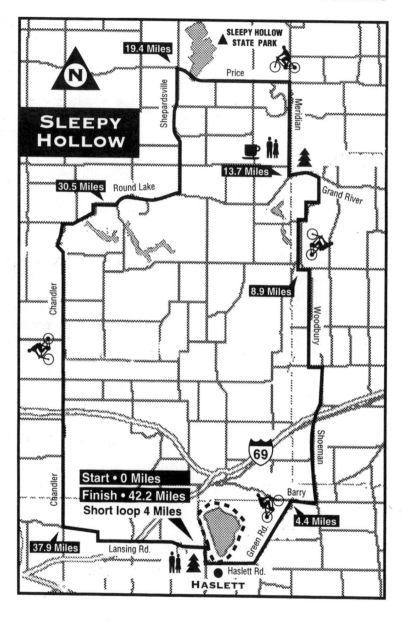

SLEEPY HOLLOW
STATE PARK

Price

19.4 Miles

N

SLEEPY
HOLLOW

Shepardsville

Meridian

13.7 Miles

Grand River

30.5 Miles   Round Lake

8.9 Miles

Woodbury

Chandler

69

Shoeman

Chandler

Barry

Start • 0 Miles
Finish • 42.2 Miles
Short loop 4 Miles

4.4 Miles

Green Rd.

37.9 Miles   Lansing Rd.

Haslett Rd.

HASLETT

willow tree, and takes you down a steep hill at **Mile 6**. The road is nicely paved with gravel shoulders, although it's a gets a bit bumpy in spots. Woodbury curves to your right near the I-69 exchange and, although the road is wide, it can be a busy corner (*careful!*).

You'll make your way uphill by the I-69 exchange at **Mile 7**. There are paved shoulders on both sides of the road. In less than a half mile, you'll certainly enjoy a nice, loonnng downhill. Before you pass Stoll Road, there are paved shoulders on both sides (yeah!). Turn right (east) onto Bath Road, a wide, two-lane road with gravel shoulders. The road will jog a bit before you will turn left (north) back on Woodbury Road at **Mile 8.9**, a stretch that takes you towards Laingsburg.

A variety of homes, open country and a large pond at **Mile 11** spice up this section of Woodbury Road, which features mostly gravel shoulders. You'll pass Britton Road and Winegar Road, travel by wildflowers, farms, lots of trees and then go over a narrow bridge in a half mile. This is followed by the Lansing Sportsman Club to your right before the road curves twice and goes through yet another residential area at **Mile 13**.

Yeah, you're in Laingsburg! The Laingsburg Town Plaza with a bakery, hot food to go, an IGA store and a pharmacy will be on your left. Turn left (west) at the 4-way stop onto Grand River Road (still in Shiawassee County, although not for long). At **Mile 13.7**, you'll enter Laingsburg, a pleasant looking small town with tree-lined streets. Laingsburg High School will be on your left followed by Nick's Pizza (for pizza, subs, salads and tacos) and a gas station if your tires need air.

Turn right (north) onto West Street to reach Bates Scout Park, operated by the City of Laingsburg. The park includes vault toilets, running water, two pavillions, picnic tables and lots of playground equipment. This is a good place to stop and enjoy a picnic lunch.

Stage two (7.2 miles) After looping through the park, turn left out of the park. Head right (north) on Meridian Road, which is the north-south dividing line between Clinton and Shiawassee counties. This flat, two-lane road travels through open farm land and has a mixture of grassy and gravel shoulders. You'll notice a sign pointing to Sleepy Hollow State Park to your left

Lake Ovid is the main feature of Sleepy Hollow State Park, located north of Lansing.

before you make a left (west) onto Price Road at **Mile 17**. Price Road is a fun one as it's lightly travelled with a couple of downhills followed by some loonnng uphills. You'll get in a good workout here as the road heads due west. At **Mile 19.4** you will reach Sleepy Hollow State Park, a nice place to add some mileage to this route. As you cycle through the park's entrance and pass the campground in a mile, you'll find the area sparsely wooded at first.

More than half of the park's visitors come to fish the 250-acre Lake Ovid in the center of the park, according to park officials. The lake provides excellent fishing for bluegill, perch, channel catfish, and pike to name a few. If you're on a mountain bicycle, you'll be happy to know you can ride on the more than 16 miles of trails within the park. With the mountain bike trails and 181 modern camp sites at Sleepy Hollow State Park, this route could turn into a two-day affair!

Stage three (16.3 miles) Turn right (west) out of Sleepy Hollow State Park, where Price Road is lightly traveled. Cross the bridge over Lake Ovid before the road makes a couple of curves beginning at **Mile 22.8**. Notice the abandoned white church on your right. What's a ride without some sort of abandoned building to check out? Turn left (south) at Shephardsville Road, a nice go-for-speed road with some rolling hills, smooth pavement, grassy shoulders and nice twists and curves. The roadside is sprinkled with wildflowers and a pleasing mixture of trees. There are cornfields on both sides at **Mile 24.5** before the road curves downhill to your right. On a summer afternoon, this section can offer a soothing, tranquil respite from the city with its wide expanse of open land dotted with farmhouses.

Within a mile there's a short, steep hill followed by more rolling hills on Shephardsville Road. At **Mile 26.5**, turn right (west) onto Round Lake Road where you will see a red barn, cornfields, a residential area and a many species of trees. Round Lake is to your left at **Mile 27.7** followed by a party store. There are a couple of hills and sharp turns on this road and an access point to Round Lake is reached in a mile.

Turn left (south) onto Chandler Road at **Mile 30.5**. Chandler is a relatively flat road that curves to the right just before a nice straightaway for turning on the speed. There are some small rolling hills, more residences and evergreen and hardwood trees as you pass Clark, Drumheller and State roads. Continue on Chandler, which will take you back to the park. You will know you've moved closer to civilization when you reach the Lansing City Limits at **Mile 37.3**.

Stage four (4.9 miles) The last leg of this route leads back to Lake Lansing County South County Park. Turn left (east) onto Lake Lansing Road at **Mile 37.9**; this is a busy intersection. At a stop light, Lake Lansing Road will jog to your right and make a sharp left through a busy section. You'll cycle by Hagadorn Road at **Mile 39.2**. There's a country club on your left just before Okemos Road. Turn left (north) onto Marsh Road to cycle in to the entrance of Lake Lansing South County Park at **43.5 miles**. Time to stretch those legs, take a swim or hunt for your non-cycling companions at the park.

Shorter option (4 miles) Cycling around Lake Lansing makes for a leisurely 4-mile loop for beginners. From Lake Lansing South County Park turn left onto Lake Lansing Road, right onto Shaw Road and veer left to Lake Drive which circles the lake back to Marsh Road. This short lakeshore loop will also give you a chance to explore the 410-acre Lake Lansing North County Park, on the northeast side of the lake.

Bicycle sales, service

Central Park Bicycles, 1805 Central Park, Okemos; ☎ (517) 349-8880.

Denny's Cycling & Fitness, 5023 W. Saginaw, Lansing; ☎ (517) 321-6700; 1215 E. Grand River Ave., East Lansing; ☎ (517) 351-2000 and 143 N. Harrison, East Lansing: ☎ (517) 332-8655.

Discount Peddler, 121 E. Kalamazoo St., Lansing; ☎ (517) 372-8088.

Don's Bicycle Services - Bike-A-Van, 1531 Jerome, Lansing: ☎(517) 372-2122.

Eric's Bicycle Shop, 6070 S. Logan, Lansing; ☎ (517) 882-7003.

Puck & Pedal Pro Shop, 326 Morgan Lane, Lansing; ☎ (517) 332-6677.

Riverfront Cycles, 507 E. Shiawassee, Lansing; ☎ (517) 482-8585 or (517) 484-0362.

Velocipede Peddler, 539 E. Grand River, East Lansing; ☎ (517) 351-7240.

Area attractions

See River Trail tour for additional attractions in the Lansing and East Lansing area.

Rose Lake Wildlife Research Center; ☎ (517) 373-9358.

Grand River Park; ☎ (517) 676-6109 or (517) 676-2233.

Area festivals, events

May: East Lansing Art Fair.

June: Downtown Lansing Art Fair.

August: Michigan Festival, Michigan State University, East Lansing.

July, August: Ingham County Fair, Mason.

September: Riverfest, Lansing.

Travel information

Greater Lansing Visitors Bureau, ☎ (517) 487-6800.
Lake Lansing County Parks; ☎ (517) 676-2233.
Sleepy Hollow State Park; ☎ (517) 651-6217.

Cycling Trip Tip #9

It's possible to stretch on a bike, especially during long rides when you're trying to minimize the number of breaks you take. Each half hour, stand and pedal for a minute. Then coast and, while still standing, rotate your hips forward while arching your back. You can also do slow neck rolls, a series of shoulder shrugs or vary your hand position to ease the grip on the handlebars. All this will assist you in overcoming upper body fatigue that comes from remaining in a rigid position.

When you do stop use your breaks to get off the bike, stretch your legs and have something to eat. But try to avoid breaks longer than 10 minutes if you have a long day ahead of you and don't snack too much as it will be difficult to resume your pace.

⟨15⟩
Chippewa Country

Trip Card

Starting Point: Mt. Pleasant
County: Isabella
Distance: 46 miles
Shorter option: 15 miles
Terrain: mostly flat, some rolling hills
Highlights: Central Michigan University, farmland, antique shops in Blanchard
Suggested riders: intermediate

Maybe you're dropping off your son for his freshman year of college. Maybe you're in town for homecoming or you're going to take part in a week-long summer conference. Anyway you look at it, you've found yourself at Central Michigan University in Mt. Pleasant, smack dab in the middle of the mitten.

Have a few hours to enjoy the countryside? There's no better way than a **46-mile bicycling route** that begins at CMU's Rose Arena, home of the Chippewas.

I'm a little partial to Mt. Pleasant because I'm a graduate of CMU. We used to joke that the only mountain in Mt. Pleasant was a bump in the landscape in front of CMU's science building. After cycling the route recommended by local cyclists, I was pleasantly surprised to find that there are some rolling hills in the area. You just have to hop on your 12-speed and pedal past picturesque farms to Blanchard Road.

Although there are no mountains, Mt. Pleasant is appropriately named as it's a pleasant college town. CMU's 16,000 plus students are the economic and energizing force of the town; there are plenty of pizza joints, more than its share of bars and, of course, eateries for after your ride.

The campus itself is compact and nice to pedal through, especially on a weekend or in the summer when the campus quiets down to a murmur. From its beginning as a small business school, CMU took on an important role in teacher preparation for the State of Michigan. Today CMU, a state university since 1897, is a complex educational institution, preparing students for a variety of careers and professions, including writing biking books!

Besides the campus, the other highlight of this ride is Blanchard, a small town at the end of stage two of the ride. The town is brimming with antiques housed in quaint stores with names like Auntie's House Antique and Country Gifts, Loafer's Glory Antique, Johnson Junque Timeless Treasures and Calico Corner Creative Country Pottery, all on a street suited for strolling after you lock up your bicycles. In case you get hungry there's a grocery store, a restaurant and an ice cream parlor here before you make the second half of your journey back to the CMU campus.

Stage one (10.8 miles) Park in the Rose Arena parking lot, East Lot, a large parking area in a convenient location on the south end of campus near the football stadium on Broomfield Road. At the stop sign, head left (west) on Broomfield, a wide road with a grassy boulevard in the middle. Careful, the road here can be busy; it's wide but has no shoulders. Very shortly you will leave CMU's campus. The road narrows to two lanes at **Mile 1**, where there are gravel shoulders. You'll find a nursery on your left and a golf center within a half mile and then at **Mile 2.5** you'll pass the Whitehead Farm, one of several farms in this largely agricultural county.

The road curves sharply to your left (south) and becomes Whiteville Road, a narrow, lightly travelled road between trees and open farmland. There are no shoulders on the road until you

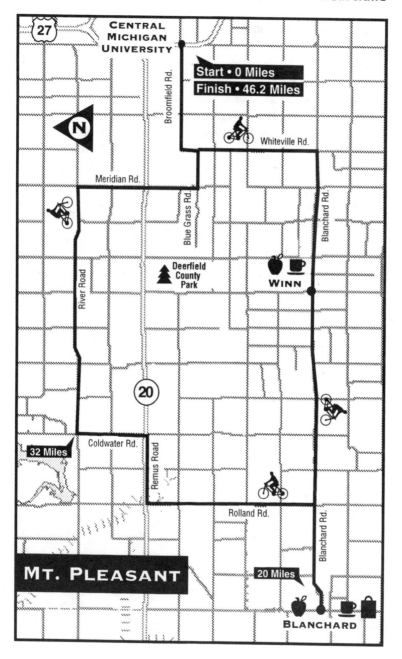

27

CENTRAL MICHIGAN UNIVERSITY

Broomfield Rd.

Start • 0 Miles
Finish • 46.2 Miles

N

Whiteville Rd.

Meridian Rd.

Blue Grass Rd.

Blanchard Rd.

River Road

Deerfield County Park

WINN

20

Coldwater Rd.

32 Miles

Remus Road

Rolland Rd.

Blanchard Rd.

MT. PLEASANT

20 Miles

BLANCHARD

pass a picturesque farm at **Mile 4**. After a couple of curves through more farmland, you will notice a quaint, two-story log house on your left at 5.2 miles followed by a medium-sized hill. Then there are rolling hills on this quiet road.

You'll pass by an abandoned church on your left at **Mile 6**, something that always adds a little character and intrigue to a long road tour. Shortly after, you'll travel through a stretch of rolling hills and then pass a horse farm. Turn right (west) onto Blanchard Road at **Mile 7**. The road starts out flat but if you like hills, you won't be disappointed. Within a half mile there's a nice section of trees followed by wide, open farmland. The road becomes a little bumpy at **Mile 8.4**, and there are still no shoulders.

Here come those rolling hills. There's a gradual uphill beginning at **Mile 8.9** followed by a large red barn and hilly stretch through more scenic, open farmland. There is a *Welcome to Winn* sign at **Mile 10.4** and, as you've probably guessed, Winn is a small town.

The Judge's Bench, a small-town bar with a homey atmosphere, was a favorite hangout of my brother and his friends, also CMU graduates, who frequented it to get away from the *big* town of Mt. Pleasant and, of course, to enjoy cheap beer. The bar is in the heart of Winn at 2603 Blanchard Rd. ☎ (517-866-2450). Pat, the owner, sells all kinds of food there including hamburgers, chicken, fish and steak. There's also a shopping center with a small grocery store in town.

Stage two (9.2 miles) Cycle west on Blanchard Road out of town where you'll come to a four-way stop at South Winn Road. Keep heading west, where there's a mix of gravel and grassy shoulders. Slightly rolling hills begin at **Mile 11.7**. and a weather-beaten barn is passed within a mile (how's that for character?). The route moves into open country where you'll undoubtedly enjoy the long, gradual downhill beginning at **Mile 13.4**, followed by a gradual uphill. After a small store is reached at **Mile 15**, you encounter more rolling, rolling hills. The road is narrow in spots here, so watch the traffic closely.

There are more hills and a semi-wooded area on both sides of the road at **Mile 16.4**, followed by more hills in the next mile. After this you will need to be careful as the road curves sharply over the hills. At **Mile 19.4** you reach Blanchard Area Parks & Recreation area. There are more sharp turns, dirt and grassy shoulders and one last sharp right before you cycle through a residential section near downtown Blanchard at **Mile 20**.

Here you'll find a street full of antique stores which sell small crafts and collectibles that could easily be packed in your bike bag. There's a grocery store for quick snacks. Loafer's Glory at 431 Main St., is open primarily for lunch and serves up homemade bread and fine desserts in its tea house and has a cozy ice cream parlor.

Stage three (16.1 miles) All rested up and ready to roll? Backtrack east on Blanchard Road pedalling the hills in the opposite direction. Turn left (north) onto South Rolland Road at **Mile 22.9**. This is another lightly travelled road, narrow with no shoulders. It's open country as you cross a bridge over a creek at **Mile 24.3**. Watch out for the bumps as you make your way uphill. There are a couple of curves and then a tunnel of trees going downhill at about **Mile 25** followed by more hills. There are no shoulders on the road here but it's lightly travelled. The road is a bit bumpy before you make a right (east) on Remus Road (M-20) at **Mile 28**. Remus Road can be very busy but has paved or gravel shoulders.

Just beyond **Mile 29.2**, you'll come across one of those treats you could not enjoy fully in an automobile: farmland for miles on all sides! At **Mile 30**, turn left (north) onto Coldwater Road, another narrow road with gravel shoulders. This road begins with a hill followed by wide open country as you cycle past a large farm. Turn right (east) onto West River Road at **Mile 32**. West River Road is narrow, with both gravel and grassy shoulders. After cornfields, you'll cycle by a Christmas tree farm and cross the Chippewa River at **Mile 33.3**. The road makes a few more curves before it flattens out as you pass Winn Road and complete your third stage at **Mile 36**.

Although there's no business establishment here, this might be a good spot to stop and catch your breath and munch on those M&M's you bought in Blanchard.

Stage four (10.1 miles) Now you're on the last leg back to Mt. Pleasant. If you want to add mileage, you can cycle approximately 3 miles south on Winn Road to Deerfield County Park, a well-kept secret run by Deerfield Township, the Mt. Pleasant School District, and the Boy Scouts. College students have long used the park as a getaway. The pleasant park includes trails for hiking, if you're so inclined, and shelters, tables and grills for a picnic break. Along the 7.5-mile network of trails, there are many scenic spots overlooking the Chippewa River and a wooden, covered bridge.

Continue cycling east on River Road where you'll cross a narrow bridge at **Mile 37.3**. The road curves sharply to your right, then to your left before you cross Meridian Road within 2 miles. Turn right onto South Lincoln Road, a narrow road with dirt shoulders. You will pass by more farmland, a residential area and a housing development before you cross M-20, a busy intersection at **Mile 43.3**. You're now just west of CMU's campus. There's a narrow bridge right before you cross the Chippewa River again. Turn left onto busy East Broomfield at **Mile 44.3**.

You'll pass the Mt. Pleasant City Limits sign in a half mile. The sign says "Still Partying After 59 Years". That slogan refers to The Cabin, a popular bar and eatery at the edge of campus at **Mile 45.6**.

Near the edge of campus, you'll find a 7-11 store on your left followed by "The Towers", a set of four dorms. The Towers are the tallest buildings in Mt. Pleasant, topping out at eight stories. They stick a lot of the freshmen in "The Towers", which have the reputation of being quite rowdy. The Rose Arena parking lot is to your right at **Mile 46.2**.

The highlight of a stop at Deerfield County Park is a stroll across its covered bridge.

You don't have to worry about lack of food choices after your ride. Every imaginable type of fast food can be bought on Mission Road, Mt. Pleasant's main street. Locals recommend Taco Boy for Mexican food on Preston Street, just off of Mission Road, or The Embers on Mission Road, which has a long tradition of fine dining for middle Michigan.

Shorter option (15.3 miles) From the Rose Arena parking lot, turn west onto Broomfield Road. The road curves sharply to your left and becomes Whiteville Road. Turn right (west) onto Blue Grass Road, then right (north) onto Meridian Road. Cross the Chippewa River and pass Meridian Park, before you cross M-20. Turn right (east) on River Road and take a right (south) onto South Lincoln. Turn left (east) onto East Pickard, right (south) onto Harris, and then left (east) to Broadway by Nelson Park, a park with a live, caged black bear, deer and badger. There are also restrooms and picnic facilities here.

Turn right (south) onto University Avenue, right (west) onto Bellows Street and left (south) onto Washington. Finally, turn left (east) onto Broomfield Road. This shorter option takes you through the heart of CMU's campus.

Bicycle sales, service

Foltz Bike Shop, 4992 E. Pickard, Mt. Pleasant; ☎ (517) 772-0183.

Motorless Motion, 121 S. Main, Mt. Pleasant; ☎ (517) 772-2008.

Area attractions

Deerfield County Park; ☎ (517) 772-2879.
Saginaw Chips Casino, Mt. Pleasant; ☎ (800) 338-9092.

Area events, festivals

June: Summer Festival; Co-Expo World Championship Rodeo, Mt. Pleasant.

July: Sawmill Days, Weidman; Antique Car Show, Blanchard

August: Isabella County Fair, Mt. Pleasant; Antique Car & Steam Engine Show, Blanchard.

September: Wheatland Music Festival, Remus.

Travel information

Isabella County Convention & Visitors Bureau; ☎ (800) 77-CHIEF or (517) 772-4433.

Cycling Trip Tip #10

The only way to keep that new bicycle looking forever new is to never ride it, something most of us can't afford to do. But remember that wet bikes rust. After every ride make an effort to wipe the mud and moisture of yours. Also remember that sunshine and oil rot rubber. Park bikes in the shade and avoid oil spots on dirt roads and pavement.

Thumb And Tri-Cities

Blue Water Tour
Lexington Loop
Tip O' The Thumb
Sleeper Amble
Little Bavaria Tour
Showboat Cruise
Bay Area Tour
Maple Syrup Ride

Fort Gratiot Light, Port Huron's historic lighthouse on Lake Huron.

16

Blue Water Tour

Trip Card

Starting Point: Lakeport State Park
County: St. Clair
Distance: 41 miles
Terrain: flat with some moderate hills
Highlights: Lakeport State Park, Ruby Farms
Suggested riders: intermediate

At the end of I-94, across the border from Sarnia, Ontario, is Port Huron (population 34,000), the hub of the Blue Water region. The most recognized feature of this city is the Blue Water Bridge, spanning the St. Clair River to link the U.S. to Canada.

Constructed in 1937, the bridge offers a panoramic view of the entire 33 miles of the river, which flows from Lake Huron into Lake St. Clair. Naturally with all the water, Port Huron hosts many wet events including the famous Port Huron to Mackinac Race in mid-July. The international atmosphere, the waterfront, museums and other attractions and amenities make the Blue Water region a fine destination for cycling.

This cycling route begins north of Port Huron at Lakeport State Park on Lake Huron and explores country roads southwest of the park. Near the small town of Ruby you can pet a deer, sip cider and take a break at Ruby Farms, an interesting attraction with a jumble of delights including Christmas trees and pumpkins during the fall.

Stage one (16 miles) Lakeport State Park, located north of Port Huron on M-25, is the starting point for this 41-mile route. The 556-acre park is actually two separate units, with the day-use area and beach located south of village of Lakeport and it's 315-site campground to the north. The park's main attraction is its wide sandy beach, and a good place to park is the picnic area of the day-use unit on the west side of M-25. There's a pedestrian walkway over the state highway to reach the beach before or after your ride.

Keep in mind that a $4 daily vehicle permit or an $18 annual state park pass is required to park in the day-use area. There is no entry fee for those who pedal into the park.

Turn left (north) out of the park onto M-25 which will take you into the town of Lakeport. At **Mile 1.2** cycle left (west) on Burtch Road, a narrow forested road that is lightly traveled. The road makes a lot of twists and curves before it straightens out and heads west. You'll pass a pumpkin patch and some cornfields before some fun rolling hills beginning at **Mile 5**.

The Blaine General Store is reached at a four-way stop, less than a mile before you turn left (south) on Wildcat Road. This road, a bit bumpy at first, is a fun, wide open country road where you can really pick up the speed. Wildcat Road curves sharply past a series of country homes and a classic red barn before you turn left (east) on M-136 at **Mile 10.3**. This wide, two-lane road, which has a mix of paved and gravel shoulders, can be busy at times. After turning right (south) on Vincent Road at **Mile 11.5** you ride though predominatly rural scenery.

Vincent Road makes an "S" curve beginning at **Mile 14** past Sycamore Street, and then the traffic increases as you near the town of Wadhams. Watch for hidden driveways along a downhill stretch that curves to the right at **Mile 15.4**. In less than a half mile you cross the Black River, then reach the Wadhams Plaza at **Mile 16**. In this busy commercial strip there's an IGA store, French's Bakery and Cafe and Hungry Howie's Pizza & Subs, making it a good area to stop for a break.

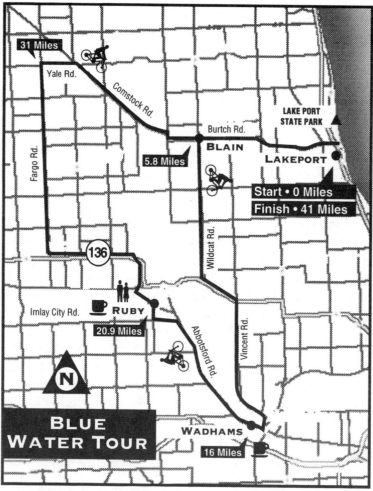

Stage two (4.9 miles) At the intersection of Vincent and Lapeer Road turn right (west) on Lapeer Road by the arrow pointing toward Ruby Farms. Be careful here. The two-lane road has dirt shoulders and the traffic can be busy as you make your way out of Wadhams. You'll pass a hardware store, the Wadhams House of Pizza and a party store before you turn right (north) on Abbotsford Road at *Mile 17.2*.

The scenery on this winding road includes log homes and

other nice houses followed by an uphill stretch that leads to a beautiful wooded section, and then Ruby Farms near **Mile 21**. The farm includes a petting zoo, cider mill, wax museum, pony and wagon rides, gift shop and restaurant. It's a great place to stop on a weekend; hours are 11 a.m. to 5 p.m. Friday, Saturday and Sunday.

Stage three (20.2 miles) Cycle left (west) out of Ruby Farms on Abbotsford Road and follow the road as it twists and turns through forested hills. At **Mile 23.2** turn left (north) on M-136. The state road features gravel shoulders and light traffic. You enter farm country before turning right (north) onto Fargo Road at **Mile 26**.

This two-lane county road is fairly level but a bit bumpy when you enter the village of Fargo. At **Mile 31**, you cycle past the Fargo Market and then turn right (east) onto Yale Road, which features a mix of gravel and paved shoulders. Yale Road makes a sharp curve southeast when Comstock Road merges into it and then heads downhill to cross the Black River at **Mile 33.6**. You cycle through two more sharp curves and finally merge into Burtch Road. You're in the home stretch now!

After passing the Blaine General Store again, you backtrack to the park along Burtch Road. Turn right (south) onto M-25 where shortly you'll reach the day-use area of Lakeport State Park at **Mile 41**. Time to relax at the sandy beach, check out a restaurant in nearby Port Huron or round up the shoppers in your group at the Birchwood Mall.

Bicycle sales, service

Alpine Cycles, 726 Huron Ave., Port Huron; ☎ (810) 982-9281.

MGM Bicycles, 2408 Griswold, Port Huron; ☎ (810) 982-3080.

Marine City Sport and Bike, 6752 River Road, Marine City; ☎ (810) 765-9042.

Area attractions

Ruby Farms, Ruby; ☎ (810) 324-2662.

Blue Water Bridge; U.S. Customs ☎ (810) 985-9541.

Mary Maxim's Exclusive Needlework & Crafts, Port Huron; ☎ (810) 987-2000.

Port Huron Museum of Arts and History, Port Huron; ☎ (810) 982-0891.

Blue Water Trolley, Port Huron; ☎ (810) 987-7373.

Area events and festivals

June: "Capture" Beach Volleyball Tournament, Michigan Log Cabin Day, Port Huron; St. Clair Art Fair, St. Clair; Pickerel Tournament, Algonac; Chippewas of Sarnia Annual Pow Wow, Sarnia, Ontario.

July: Blue Water Festival, Mackinac Sailboat Weekend, Lighted Boat Festival, Sand Sculpturing Contest, Port Huron; Sailboat Races, Port Huron to Port Sanilac; Riverbank Antique Show, Marine City; Yale Bologna Festival, Yale.

August: Gus Macker 3 on 3 Basketball Tournament, Great Cardboard Regatta, Port Huron; Maritime Days, Marine City.

September: Antique Classic Boat Show, Port Huron.

October: Autumn Fest, Octoberfest, Port Huron.

Travel information

The Blue Water Convention & Tourist Bureau; ☎ (810) 987-TOUR or (800) 852-4242.

Lakeport State Park; ☎ (810) 327-6765.

City of Port Huron Recreation Department (information on river walks in Port Huron); ☎ (810) 984-9760.

Sarnia Tourism Bureau; ☎ (800) 265-0316.

The Port Sanilac Lighthouse is one of many along the bicycle routes of East Michigan.

17

Lexington Loop

Trip Card

Starting point: Lexington
County: Sanilac
Distance: 44 miles
Shorter options: 11 miles and 23 miles
Terrain: Flat
Highlights: Lake Huron, beaches, Croswell's swinging bridge
Suggested Riders: Beginners and intermediate

Heading north into the Thumb region of Michigan along M-25, the first county you enter is Sanilac and the first town is delightful Lexington. Founded in 1855, this lakeside port boomed at the turn of the century and boasted 2,400 residents, due in part to Great Lakes shipping, an organ factory, a brewery, a flour mill and six saloons. Count 'em six.

Today the organ factory is gone and so is the brewery but thanks to its past Lexington has become a lively summer haven for anglers, sun bathers, tourists and, yes, cyclists. The town of 800 features streets lined with 19th century homes and mansions, many of them now bed and breakfasts, and four buildings listed on the National Register of Historic Places. Toss in Lexington's interesting harbor, its great beach and a main street of small shops and cafes and you have the reason why many cyclists like to begin and end a trip here.

This 44-mile route also passes through Croswell, home of the

Be-Good-To-Your-Mother-In-Law Bridge (I kid you not), and Port Sanilac, another delightful and historic Lake Huron community. In between the towns, the ride is level for the most part along rural county roads with extremely light traffic. The exception is M-90 between Lexington and Croswell, which is avoided by using a paved bike path.

You also pedal 16 miles on M-25, passing excellent views of Lake Huron along the way. While the road can be busy at times, especially on the weekends with families heading to or from their cottages, the 11-mile stretch between Port Sanilac and Lexington was recently resurfaced and features wide, paved shoulders.

Stage one (5.5 miles) The ride begins at the east end of Huron Street in Lexington at Pat Tierney Park and beach adjacent to Lexington Harbor. The park features a parking area, picnic tables, grills, restrooms and other facilities. Head west on Huron Street, immediately climbing a hill into downtown Lexington and then carefully cross busy M-25 to continue on Huron Street.

Within 0.6 mile you reach the edge of town where Huron Street turns into M-90 and a bicycle path begins. The asphalt-paved path parallels M-90 for the next five miles and at **Mile 1.2**, you begin climbing a gradual but *loooong* slope that is sometimes referred to as Shamrock Hill. The climb lasts a half mile, and once you've reached the top the scenery becomes a series of farms, barns and orchards.

At **Mile 4.7** you enter Croswell and the bike path swings north on Howard Street briefly before ending. A wide concrete sidewalk takes over and takes you into "downtown" Croswell. Within a quarter mile you turn west on Sanborn Avenue, immediately cross the Black River and then turn north on Nims Street to reach the *Be-Good-To-Your-Mother-In-Law* Bridge Park. Within the park there are picnic tables, a pavilion, drinking water, vault toilets and that swing bridge which bounces and sways with every step you take across it. It's the number one attraction in Croswell.

Backtrack to Sanborn Avenue and continue west to quickly

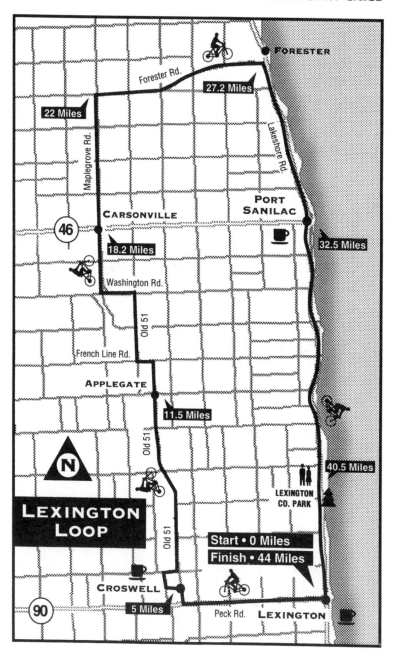

FORESTER

Forester Rd.

27.2 Miles

22 Miles

Maplegrove Rd.

Lakeshore Rd.

PORT
SANILAC

CARSONVILLE

(46)

32.5 Miles

18.2 Miles

Washington Rd.

Old 51

French Line Rd.

APPLEGATE

11.5 Miles

Old 51

40.5 Miles

N

LEXINGTON
CO. PARK

LEXINGTON
LOOP

Old 51

Start • 0 Miles
Finish • 44 Miles

CROSWELL

(90)

5 Miles

Peck Rd. LEXINGTON

reach Black River Drive. Head north and then apply the brakes at Croswell Berry Farm at **Mile 5.5** if you're hungry or thirsty. The farm is best known for its "pick your own" fields of blackberries, raspberries, strawberries and blueberries. But there is also a small cafe here that serves soup and sandwiches from 11 a.m. to 3 p.m., and ice cream and slices of Berry-Berry-Cherry pie (black and red raspberries mixed with cherries) all day from 8 a.m. to 6 p.m. during the summer.

Stage two (12.7 miles) Head north on Black River Drive, a well-packed dirt road and in a half mile you arrive at Harrington Road. Turn east (right) on Harrington to re-cross the Black River and then north (left) on N. Howard Avenue to depart Croswell.

On most maps North Howard is labeled Sherman but along the road itself it's usually posted as Old 51. At **Mile 11.5** you enter the village of Applegate, the site of a few antique shops, including an interesting one called The Bank, and a party store. Continue north along Old 51, a level country road with narrow shoulders but little traffic, and follow it as the road makes an "S" curve to the west at **Mile 12.7** and again at **Mile 15.4**, where you follow Washington Road briefly before continuing north. At both places the set of double curves are clearly marked and there is little doubt as to which road to follow.

From here you head due north and in 3 miles pedal into the village of Carsonville at **Mile 18.2**. This is a sleepy little junction in the middle of the county where you'll find a couple of small grocers.

Stage three (14.3 miles) In Carsonville, Old 51 becomes Main Street, and as you head north out of town it turns into Maple Grove Road. Again the road features narrow shoulders and light traffic but does have a few mild slopes to contend with. Nothing to work up a sweat over though.

Within 4 miles of Carsonville at **Mile 22.2** you arrive at a stop sign and turn east (right) on Forester Road. Here you actu-

The Be-Good-To-Your-Mother-In-Law Bridge, in the heart of Croswell along the Lexington Loop bike tour.

ally experience a few hills in the next 2 miles and then Forester Road veers to the left, splitting away from Day Road, which is dirt. Continue on Forester Road through an area of both farm fields and stands of trees and at **Mile 27.7** the road ends at M-25 in the village of Forester, where you'll find a party store.

Head south (right) along M-25. The state highway is badly in need of resurfacing for the next 5 miles and maybe by the time you undertake this trip it will be done. You'll also find gravel shoulders and considerably heavier traffic than on the last 20 miles. But you can't beat the view. Just south of Forester is a half-mile stretch where you have a sweeping panorama of Lake Huron from the edge of a lakeshore bluff.

Port Sanilac is reached 5 miles south of Forester at **Mile 32.5**. This is another historical community although not nearly as "touristy" as Lexington. Within town there are a couple of ice cream shops and the Sanilac Bakery and Deli. On the south side of town, next door to each other on M-25, are a couple of interesting restaurants. The Bellaire Lodge features steaks and seafood but if you feel too self-conscious about entering it in your biking shorts, then try Palermo's Stone Lodge. It's something of an out-of-place sports bar that has beer on tap and big hamburgers sizzling on the grill.

Also take time to swing off M-25 onto Lake Street along Lake Huron to see the picturesque Port Sanilac Lighthouse. Commissioned in 1886, the white tower is 59 feet tall and crowned in red. It's adjoined to a red brick lighthouse keeper's residence and today is operated by the U.S. Coast Guard. If your timing is right, more area history can be viewed at the Sanilac County Historical Museum just south of town on M-25. From mid-June through Labor Day it's open Tuesday through Sunday. There is a small admission fee.

Stage four (11.5 miles) At Port Sanilac M-25 turns into a beautifully paved road with extra wide paved shoulders sure to please even the most diehard cyclist. Within a mile south of town you arrive at a rest area overlooking Lake Huron from the edge of a bluff and featuring tables, drinking water and vault toilets. There is also an historical marker here dedicated to the Great Storm of 1913 that sank 10 ships on the Great Lakes including eight on Lake Huron.

At **Mile 37** you pass another great view of Lake Huron and at **Mile 40.5** you arrive at the day-use area entrance of Lexington Park. Open 8 a.m. to dusk, the park features picnic tables, restrooms, water and a pavilion in case it's raining. If it isn't, there is also a nice beach here to cool off any overheated cyclist.

Lexington is just another 3.5 miles down the road, the end of this 44-mile pedal. Take a dip at the beach in Pat Tierney Park where you started or satisfy a post-ride hunger at A&W, Dairy Queen and Smackwater Jack's for subs and sandwiches to name just a few. If you're into quaint shops, check out the Lexington General Store.

Shorter Option (11 or 23 miles) If you have children in your party and need a shorter ride, the bike path between Lexington and Croswell makes for an excellent trip. You stay away from any roads and the young ones can bounce on Croswell's famous swinging bridge before heading back to complete the 11-mile round trip.

The stretch between Lexington and Port Sanilac is also a good 23-mile ride along a road that you won't mind backtracking.

Bicycle sales, service

Alpine Cycles, 726 Huron Ave., Port Huron; ☎ (810) 982-9281.

MGM Bicycles, 2408 Griswold, Port Huron; ☎ (810) 982-3080.

Area Attractions

Sanilac County Historical Museum, ☎ (810) 622-9949.
Croswell Berry Farm, ☎ (810) 679-3273

Area Events And Festivals

May: Blessing of the Fleet, Port Sanilac.
June: Pioneer Days, Croswell.
July: Fourth of July, Lexington and Port Sanilac; Summer Festival, Port Sanilac; Agricultural Fair, Croswell.
August: Lexington Art Fair; Port Sanilac Art Show.

Travel information

Lexington Chamber of Commerce, ☎ (810) 359-2262.

Cycling Trip Tip #11

For two to three days before a long ride (50 miles or more) or a multi-day tour, eat carbohydrate-rich foods such as pasta, rice or potatoes. Your body will quickly convert the carbohydrates into glycogen, the energy needed while cycling.

The Garfield Inn, where President James Garfield once stayed, is a delightful bed and breakfast in Port Austin.

⟨18⟩

Tip O' The Thumb

Trip Card

Starting point: Port Crescent State Park
County: Huron
Distance: 44.4 miles
Shorter option: 15 miles
Terrain: flat, slight hills
Highlights: Port Austin, Huron City, Lighthouse Park, Lake Huron
Suggested riders: beginners to intermediate

Detroiters can load bikes onto their cars and head straight north on M-53, and in less than three hours (even less for Flint and Saginaw residents) reach a special place. It's an area full of simple charms, where you can take a leisurely walk on a sandy beach, camp at two accessible state parks or just slow down and enjoy life. Welcome to the tip of the Thumb, outlined by Saginaw Bay to the west and Lake Huron to the east.

Often called the getaway close to home for many Michigan urban areas, the Thumb offers a slower, simpler way of life and a respite from the city. The charm of the region is that your needs are minimal; there are plenty of scenic roads for touring, cozy cottages, hiking areas, restaurants and party stores and sandy beaches along the Lake Huron shoreline. What more do you need?

Lately cyclists have discovered M-25 in the Thumb. With wide shoulders, the road closely follows Lake Huron and is a natural for road bikes. And you only have to turn inland, away from the lake, to find a rich rural area, with flat, open roads suitable for picking up speed. These roads are nicely laid out, more or less in grids.

Variety spices up this 44-mile route. Along the lakeshore areas there's a forget-your-troubles atmosphere with a host of different types of cottages, small motels and bed & breakfasts. The small town of Port Austin has typical tourist stuff but it's unpretentious, a good place for a break with its eateries, a marina for watching boats and an old-fashioned dime store. Rounding the tip of the Thumb you'll see the much-photographed lighthouse in Lighthouse Park, a nice stop halfway into the route.

Travelers often bypass, or should I say sideswipe, the Thumb as a destination, because it doesn't pass through to somewhere else. Fishermen and hunters have long sought out the waters and woods of the tip of the Thumb. Maybe it's time for you (and your bicycle) to check it out, too!

Stage one (7.6 miles) A convenient place to begin this loop is at the day use area of Port Crescent State Park, a park with the largest sand dunes and beaches on the east side of Michigan. The panoramic views from the wind-swept dunes of the state park encompass miles of shoreline and a valley carved by the Pinnebog River. After cycling your way out of the park on a tree-lined road, turn left onto M-25. Careful: this main byway of the area can be busy, although the shoulders are nicely paved. All levels of cyclists will enjoy M-25.

You cross over the Pinnebog River at **Mile 1.1**. The road follows the curve of the tip of the Thumb and as you make your way toward Port Austin you'll pass a nice tree-lined section full of evergreens and hardwoods. Cycle by the Bucaneer Inn Dining and Lodging on your left at **Mile 2.4** before passing the entrance to the Port Crescent State Park campground. (Rummage sales are plentiful in many parts of East Michigan. Don't forget to pack your spare change and leave room in your bike bag for bargains.)

There is still a well paved shoulder as you wind your way past a collection of cottages, small motels and beachfront homes on M-25. At **Mile 4.2**, on your left you'll cycle by Jenks Park on the lake, another possible starting point for this ride. You can tell you're getting closer to Port Austin because of the increased number of homes and cottages. There's a market on your left, a mixture of wildflowers, cottages on both sides of the road and many trees. You cross the Port Austin village limits at **Mile 6.5**. Tur-

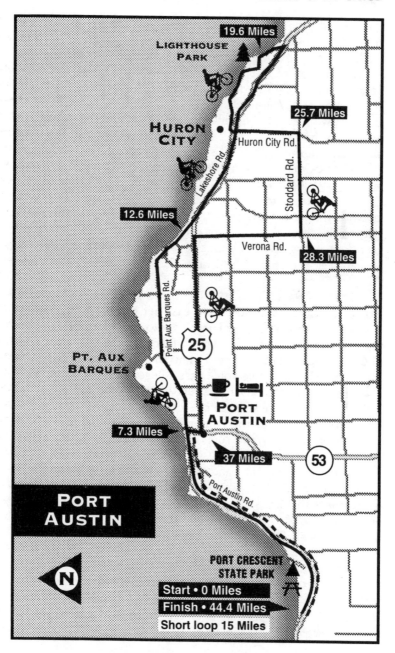

19.6 Miles

25.7 Miles

LIGHTHOUSE PARK

HURON CITY

Huron City Rd.

Lakeshore Rd.

Stoddard Rd.

12.6 Miles

Verona Rd.

28.3 Miles

Point Aux Barques Rd.

US 25

PT. AUX BARQUES

PORT AUSTIN

7.3 Miles

37 Miles

53

Port Austin Rd.

PORT AUSTIN

N

PORT CRESCENT STATE PARK

Start • 0 Miles

Finish • 44.4 Miles

Short loop 15 Miles

quoise and yellow signs let you know you are welcome in this town. As you make your way into the downtown area, watch for traffic, although no one seems to be in a hurry during the summer. At the junction of M-53 and M-25 (notice the green and white Lake Huron Circle Tour sign) there's public access for boats, and boat watching at **Mile 7.3**.

In town the road becomes Spring Street and the downtown area is to the right. At this point the road widens and there are sidewalks on the right hand side of the road, but no shoulders. Bird Creek County Park, a delightful public beach and boardwalk, will be to your left within a third of a mile. Maybe it's time to stop for a break to watch the boats, lock the bikes and take a walk downtown. You can enjoy Port Austin now or later as this route backtracks through here. Take a quick look around - there are plenty of eating choices, shops to browse through or spots at which to sit and enjoy the scenery.

Stage two (12 miles) The name of the road changes to Point Aux Barques as you cycle east out of Port Austin, where there's more open country. There's a mixture of farmland to your right and lots of trees to your left following the lake after **Mile 8.6**. This two-lane road either has no shoulders and or just gravel shoulders. Within a mile you'll pass a huge cornfield on the right and then a golf course on the left. At this point you enter flat, open country where you can see for miles.

A nice size hill for this route crests at **Mile 10.7** followed by a relatively steep downhill run. The road makes a few sharp curves beginning at **Mile 12**, and in just over one-half mile you'll notice a recreational vehicle park and marina and the Grindstone Bar & Grill to your left. Tiny Grindstone City was named after huge grindstones that are still on the beach from when the town, with its abundance of natural sandstone, produced most of the world's grinding wheels. The owner of the Grindstone Bar & Grill can give you an oral history of the area, while serving you what's been reported as the best hamburger in the Thumb.

The road curves to the right and becomes Pearson Road near **Mile 13**. This two-lane road, with farmland on both sides, ends at M-25, a byway that pops up a lot on this route. Cycle to the left on M-25 beginning at **Mile 13.6**. This section of M-25 can also be busy but there are nicely paved shoulders on both sides of the road. South M-25 at this point is called Lakeshore Road. There's a long gradual downhill for picking up speed before you cross over the New River in less than 2 miles. You'll pass the New River Cemetery, a scenic cemetery on a small hillside. At **Mile 17**, you'll want to cycle left onto Huron City Road where you can stop and enjoy the Thumb's most famous attraction - Huron City.

Huron City, a prosperous lumbering town in the mid-1800's, barely survived the Great Fire of 1881. Before the fire, it was the largest town in the county with lumbermen producing 80,000 board-feet of lumber per day. After the fire, which ended the logging era in the Thumb, the town became a farming community and withered away to a ghost town in the early 1900's.

Huron City returned to life in the 1920s when the charismatic William Lyon Phelps, a Yale professor and an ordained minister, attracted hordes of summer visitors to hear his Sunday sermons. His granddaughter has since preserved the community as a museum town. The town's 12 buildings include a country store, the church, a lifesaving station, a settler's cabin, the old inn, a barn with antique farm equipment and the Phelps Museum. Huron City is open July 1 through Labor Day. There is an admission fee to see it.

To continue cycling, turn right onto Pioneer Road, which veers to your left and becomes Lighthouse Road. The road twists and curves with a stand of birch trees to your left as you cycle up and down a couple of hills. This picturesque road winds past a lot of trees and cottages near Lake Huron. You'll notice a barn with three gables at **Mile 18.6** followed by a home with stone fencing and an old mansion right near the water's edge. Within a mile the road curves sharply to your left into Lighthouse Park.

Lighthouse County Park is home to a picturesque lighthouse, built in 1857, which houses a small museum on the first floor. The lighthouse is still used by the U.S. Coast Guard to guide ships. The park features a 74-site campground with electricity for RVs, a swimming beach, boat launch, nature trail and a picnic area. Although there's not much in the way of sandy beach, many of the camping spots are right on the water's edge in this lush, green park. There's actually another park here - underwater! The Thumb Area Bottomland Preserve, set up by the state in 1985, protects

The lighthouse museum at Lighthouse Park in Huron County at the Tip O' The Thumb.

nine known shipwrecks. Relics from the wrecks are stored in the lighthouse museum.

The park is a nice place to walk around, stretch those legs and take photos of your companions by the lighthouse. It's also another good starting point for this ride.

Stage three (17.5 miles) Hopefully, you'll be rested as this is the longest stretch of the ride. Cycle left out of Lighthouse County Park. The road is a two-lane with no shoulders and makes a sharp curve to your right. There's a mixture of lake views and open farmland at this point. Turn right onto M-25, where again there are nice shoulders. You'll cycle past Huron City again before making a left on Huron City Road by the red barn with the classic yellow and black smiling face!

Huron City Road is an agreeable road for cyclists; it's two-lane and lightly travelled - a good one for picking up speed. At many spots wildflowers grace the roadside and you can often see far off into the distance on the relatively, flat road.

At **Mile 25.7**, turn right onto Stoddard Road, a slightly bumpy country road with no shoulders. This road is typical of the Thumb; it's mostly flat through cornfields. In less than 3 miles, turn right onto Verona Road, a country intersection of cornfields, homes and barns. Many of the roads that intersect Verona are dirt roads, suitable for mountain bicycles. It's hard to get lost in this part of Huron Country as the roads are mostly laid out in grids.

Verona Road ends back at the now familiar M-25. At **Mile 31.4** you'll see a sign that says "20 miles to Harbor Beach" but you'll be going 5 miles the other way back to Port Austin. Shortly you'll see the Grindstone City public access to your right. Careful; M-25 can be busy here. In less than 5 miles you'll find yourself at the village limits of Port Austin. M-25 veers to your right as you head back to the quaint downtown section of Port Austin.

If you didn't stop here before, maybe now's the time. Jose's Italian Bakery serves pizza and subs along with sandwiches, baked goods and soft serve ice cream. Probably the two best known eateries, though, are the Garfield Inn and The Bank 1884.

James Garfield, the 20th president of the United States, slept at what's now called the Garfield Inn. In the 1860s, he once made a speech here endorsing Ulysses Grant for president. The national historic site is now a restaurant, bar and bed & breakfast (☎ 517-738-5254). For fine dining, The Bank 1884 restaurant (☎ 517-738-5353), on the corner of Lake and State streets, offers an historic overview of Huron County. The brick building was a financial establishment until 1957. It could be a nice place to book reservations after you've freshened up after your ride.

Take a stroll through Port Austin's old-fashioned dime store, order a treat from a soda fountain or stock up on the things you forgot from home. To head back to the Port Crescent day use area cycle through the congested tourist area and turn left on M-25 (you'll notice the Lake Huron Circle Tour signs) at **Mile 37**.

Stage four (7.3 miles) To return to the starting point, you'll backtrack on M-25. Again, this road can be busy, but the paved shoulders get wider as you cycle out of town. At **Mile 44.4**, you're back at the day use area of Port Crescent State Park, near the hiking and fitness trails.

Shorter option (15 miles) Cycle from the Port Crescent State Park day-use area east on M-25 to Port Austin, and backtrack the way you came for a leisurely 15-mile ride.

Bicycle rental

Port Austin Bike Rental, Lake Street Manor Bed & Breakfast, 8569 Lake Street (M-53), Port Austin; ☎ (517) 738-7720.

Area attractions

Tip-A-Thumb Canoe Rental, Port Austin; ☎ (517) 738-7656
Huron City Museum, Huron City; ☎ (517) 428-4123.
Huron Nature Center; ☎ (517) 856-4411.

Area festivals and events

June: "On the Waterfront" Jamboree; Thumb's Up Bicycle Tour, Port Austin.

July: July 4th parade, fireworks; Open Air Artist Market, Port Austin.

Travel information

The Greater Port Austin Chamber of Commerce; ☎ (517) 738-7600.
Port Crescent State Park; ☎ (517) 738-5130.

19

Sleeper Amble

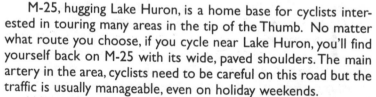

Trip Card

Starting point: Sleeper State Park
County: Huron
Distance: 32 miles
Shorter option: 10 miles round trip
Terrain: mostly flat
Highlights: Sleeper State Park, Caseville, Wild Fowl Bay, Lake Huron
Suggested riders: beginners

M-25, hugging Lake Huron, is a home base for cyclists interested in touring many areas in the tip of the Thumb. No matter what route you choose, if you cycle near Lake Huron, you'll find yourself back on M-25 with its wide, paved shoulders. The main artery in the area, cyclists need to be careful on this road but the traffic is usually manageable, even on holiday weekends.

West of Port Crescent State Park is the lesser known 1,003-acre Albert E. Sleeper State Park, your starting point for this ride. From the park, the route heads westward on M-25 and loops back around to the park through a pleasant mix of what the Thumb has to offer; rich agricultural land, a bay that's home to diverse wildlife; Caseville, a small town that welcomes visitors; an old iron bridge; and what many of us touring cyclists really enjoy - flat, paved roads for picking up the speed! Best of all, this route in the Thumb serves up a heavy dose of tranquility, an invigorating break from many of the urban areas in Michigan.

Naturally, on M-25, there are tantalizing glimpses of the lake and the sunshine peeking through many heavily wooded spots.

Except for Caseville, there aren't many places to stop for food, so you may want to pack those panniers or save your appetite for after you're finished with this 32-mile loop. You can create a feast back at the campground or enjoy a restaurant in nearby Port Austin.

Stage one (5.2 miles) From the beach parking lot of Sleeper State Park, turn right onto M-25. You'll enjoy the paved shoulders on both sides of the road as you cycle past a couple of motels on your way into Caseville. It's "Welcome to Caseville" at **Mile 3.6**, known for its fishing charters, tourist shops and homespun restaurants. The town is a haven for many nearby city dwellers from Bay City and Saginaw, and in July and August, the walleye capital of Saginaw Bay.

Just after you enter Caseville you'll cycle through a residential section and past a Dairy Queen restaurant on your left at **Mile 4.4**. Caseville County Park follows soon after, on your right. As you approach downtown Caseville you will pass a beach access, marina and ferry to your right, a trip to consider for later.

Ferries leave daily for a journey to historic Charity Island, the last uninhabited major island in the lower Great Lakes. The island features an 1857 lighthouse, ancient Indian flint quarries and miles of marked nature trails. The shoreline varies from sand to jagged rocky outcroppings.

Caseville United Methodist Church adds a graceful view at **Mile 4.7**. After you cross the Pigeon River, you've made it to the downtown area. It comes complete with a mini-market, Walt's Restaurant, gift shops and my friend Gordon's favorite restaurant (because it serves beer!), the Bluewater Inn. There's also an IGA grocery store and a fruit market if you're looking for an early break.

Cyclists need to be careful as they venture through the downtown area; the road can be busy and the paved shoulders turn into sidewalks.

Stage two (7 miles) As you cycle your way out of Caseville, the sidewalks give way to paved shoulders once again. You'll pass a Little Caesars Pizza, a cemetery, and, finally, a nice, tree-lined portion of the road at **Mile 6.3**. Don't forget to check for scenic

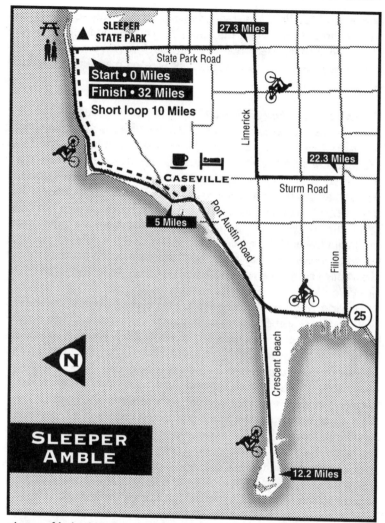

SLEEPER
STATE PARK

27.3 Miles

State Park Road

Start • 0 Miles
Finish • 32 Miles
Short loop 10 Miles

Limerick

22.3 Miles

CASEVILLE

Sturm Road

5 Miles

Port Austin Road

Filion

25

N

Crescent Beach

SLEEPER
AMBLE

12.2 Miles

views of Lake Huron which are a treat on this route.

For a fun detour, pedal Sand Point by turning right onto Crescent Beach Road at *Mile 8*. This narrow road, with paved shoulders, light traffic and lots of oak trees, is the only one on this peninsula. Sand Point is bordered by Wild Fowl Bay on the left, Saginaw Bay on right and a very scenic view at the end of this road. The road curves to your right and then left before ending at

Mile 12.2. Definitely get off those bikes, stretch your legs and enjoy the peaceful view, the rocky beach area and the birds and wildfowl that frequent the area. Although it was a holiday weekend when we cycled this route, there weren't many people around this special spot.

Stage three (13 miles) You'll notice green and white bike route signs as you backtrack on Crescent Beach Road. Turn right onto M-25 at *Mile 16.2*; watch for deer, abundant in the area. You'll cycle by more stands of stately oak trees and notice many canals to your right, where boat owners can easily navigate the waters to Saginaw Bay. Turn right onto Filion Road at *Mile 18.3*, another interesting, short detour to Wild Fowl Bay. The road has a mixture of paved and gravel shoulders. You'll enjoy scenic canals and wildflowers that grace the roadway, and possibly even stands of wild rice. In less than a half mile, there's a public access to Wild Fowl Bay. From here you backtrack on Filion Road and cross M-25 at *Mile 19*.

Filion Road is basically flat as you cycle by a golf course on your left and some Thumb area staples - corn and beans. Before you turn left onto Sturm Road at *Mile 22.3*, you'll cycle by orchards and a brick United Methodist Church. For the next 2 miles follow Sturm Road, a two-lane road with grassy or no shoulders and more prime agricultural land. Turn right onto Limerick Road where there are lots more wildflowers close to the road. On this stretch of the route, there are sugar beets to your left and right, and large expanses of farmland where you can breathe easier, relax and enjoy the countryside. There are also more cornfields before you encounter an old, one-lane iron bridge over the Pigeon River at *Mile 25.2*, a nice place to rest those muscles, take a peak at the river and marvel at the bridge's unique structure.

Stage four (6.8 miles) Turn left onto Farver Road at *Mile 27.3*. This hard-packed gravel road is still rideable with a road bicycle. After you cross Kinde Road, the road turns to pavement and becomes State Park Road, an indication you're getting closer to Sleeper State Park. This road is narrow with little traffic and lots of cornfields on both sides followed by sugar beets to your left within three miles. You'll cycle by the Country Charm Bed &

Breakfast (☎ 517-856-3110) and an outdoor center, part of Sleeper State Park, to your left at *Mile 31.2*.

The outdoor center features 16 cabins, a dining hall, a kitchen and a council ring. There are several unpaved roads to your right and left for extra mileage for those on a mountain bicycle.

Before you turn left back onto old familiar M-25, you'll pass Frank's Party Store, with the customary ice cream, beer, wine, groceries, firewood and bait! At *Mile 32*, you'll be back where you started at the parking area in Sleeper State Park. You can stretch those rubbery legs by hiking the park's 4.5-mile network of trails; there are several options available from a half-mile walk to a 2.5- mile round trip. Or simply rest by sunbathing on the half-mile of beach in Sleeper's popular day-use area.

Shorter option (10 miles) Sleeper State Park to Caseville and back makes a nice shorter option, giving beginning cyclists a destination with food, fun and gift shops as well as an occasional rummage sale to check out along the way!

Area attractions
Huron Nature Center, Sleeper State Park ☎ (517) 856-4411.

Area festivals and events
April: Caseville Perch Festival.

May: Caseville Bow Fishing Tournament.

June: Venetian Night, Caseville; Thumb's Up Bicycle Tour, Port Austin.

July: Fireworks, Caseville Craft Show and Flea Market, Caseville Auto Show, Caseville Beach Fest, Caseville.

August: Caseville Dinghy Parade.

Travel information
Caseville Chamber of Commerce; ☎ (517) 856-3818.

Frankenmuth, Michigan's Little Bavaria, features the world famous chicken dinners of the Bavarian Inn and Zenders Restaurant.

⟨20⟩
Little Bavaria Tour

Trip Card

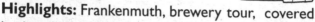

Starting point: Saginaw
County: Saginaw
Distance: 43 miles
Shorter option: 10 miles
Terrain: Flat, light traffic
Highlights: Frankenmuth, brewery tour, covered bridge, Cass River
Suggested Riders: Intermediate

Like a few hills when you cycle? Like to put your head down and pump your way up a long hill and then take a well deserved rest by gliding down the backside?

Good luck finding any in Saginaw County. Cycling doesn't get any easier than in Michigan's flattest county, basically a broad valley where several major rivers, the Flint, Cass, Shiawassee and Tittabawassee, merge on their way to Saginaw Bay.

Meandering rivers and flat terrain may be the trademark of Saginaw County but the highpoint of this 43-mile bike tour is the area's most interesting town, Frankenmuth. What began in 1845 when a group of 15 German-Lutheran missionaries arrived to convert the Chippewa Indians, has since become famed chicken dinners and the number one tourist attraction in the state. Little Bavaria is a thriving community of more than 4,000 with a bustling downtown of shops, the famous Bavarian Inn and Zehnder's restaurant across the street from each other, a cheese factory,

Michigan's oldest operating brewery, a covered bridge and Bronner's, the world's largest Christmas store.

Combine Frankenmuth with the huge Manufacturer's Mall at nearby Birch Run and it's little wonder that the stream of tour buses into this part of Saginaw County is endless.

For cyclists on a day-long ride Frankenmuth makes an interesting stop along the way, and on this route you get to pass through it twice. The Little Bavaria Tour also features pleasant country scenery, light traffic, paved roads and even a change in elevation in the form of a few gentle hills and a bluff with a sweeping view of the Cass River.

Heaven forbid! You might even have to change gears in Saginaw County.

The starting point is the YMCA in Saginaw, and to reach it you depart I-75 at exit 149B and head west on Holland Road (M-46). Stay on M-46 for several miles until it becomes Rust Avenue; just before crossing the Tittabawassee River you arrive at the YMCA, located across from the Anderson Wave Pool.

Stage one (17.6 miles) The ride begins at the YMCA parking lot. From there cyclists quickly escape city traffic by crossing Rust Avenue and heading south along Wickes Park Drive, a scenic two-mile stretch past the Tittabawassee River and the anglers trying to catch walleye from its waters.

Eventually the park road swings left (east) and ends at M-13. Continue right (south) along M-13 as it leaves the city behind. Traffic can be heavy along this stretch but M-13 has wide, paved shoulders. At **Mile 3.6** you pass a public access site and then cross the Cass River for the first of several times during the ride. At **Mile 4.3** turn left (east) on Evon Road, which in half a mile swings south into Cole Road.

Cole Road passes Spalding Township Park (picnic tables, pavilion, restrooms) and at **Mile 7.2** arrives at the intersection with Curtis Road, the only road you'll need to remember for the next 15 miles. A possible sidetrip at this point is to head right (west) on

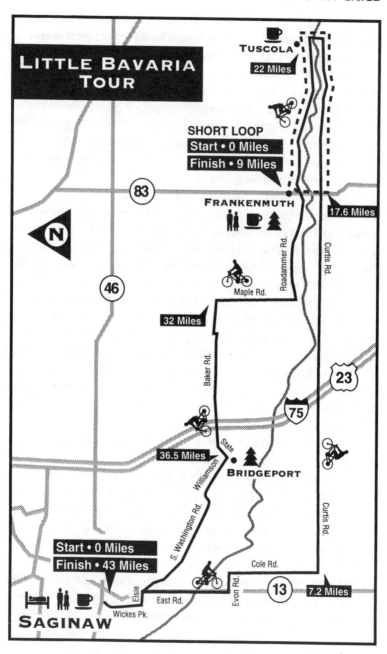

LITTLE BAVARIA
TOUR

TUSCOLA
22 Miles

SHORT LOOP
Start • 0 Miles
Finish • 9 Miles

N

83

FRANKENMUTH

17.6 Miles

Roadammer Rd.

Curtis Rd.

46

Maple Rd.

32 Miles

Baker Rd.

23

75

State

36.5 Miles

BRIDGEPORT

Williamson

Curtis Rd.

Start • 0 Miles
Finish • 43 Miles

S. Washington Rd.

Cole Rd.

Elsie

East Rd.

Evon Rd.

13

7.2 Miles

SAGINAW

Wickes Pk.

Curtis and within 2 miles you'll reach the headquarters of the Shiawassee National Wildlife Refuge, a 9,000-acre federal preserve. The headquarters is open Monday through Friday from 7:30 a.m. to 4 p.m. and can provide a map of the area and bird check list. Another 1.5 miles west of the headquarters along Curtis is the Waterfowl Trail, a 5-mile hike/bike loop that passes an observation tower and spotting scope in the heart of the refuge. In April and September, it's often possible to see thousands of ducks, herons and geese in this area. Add another 12 miles to your day if you plan to include this sidetrip.

The tour heads left (east) on Curtis from Cole Road and within a half mile you come to the stop sign and intersection at Sheridan Road and another at Blackmar Road at *Mile 11.2*. At this point Curtis becomes a typical Saginaw County road: ruler straight and flat, so flat that the biggest climb here is riding over the I-75 Bypass. But the scenery is pleasant, a country mix of corn fields, horse farms and classic red barns and silos. At *Mile 13.4* you cross Dixie Highway, *BE CAREFUL!*, and then pass lush Green Fortress Golf Course before entering Frankenmuth at *Mile 17.2*.

Main Street is reached at *Mile 17.6* and you can head north (left) here for your fill of German hospitality, fudge and quaint little shops. But an excellent meal can be had by stopping in at Kern's Sausage Shop, right there on the corner of Curtis and Main. The butchery makes its own bratwurst, liverwurst, even metwurst; you can pick up some along with sharp cheddar cheese, dark German bread and other refreshments and then head over to Heritage Park for a biker's feast. From the park you can then cross the covered bridge and be in the heart of downtown Frankenmuth.

But don't fill up on too much liverwurst and bypass the chicken dinners and the tasting tour at the Frankenmuth Brewery. You still have more than 25 miles to ride, including the most scenic stretches.

Stage two (9 miles) In Frankenmuth, Curtis becomes Jefferson Street and a third of a mile from Main Street you come to the intersection at Weiss Street. Head left (north) on Weiss to reach Heritage Park where there are bathrooms, drinking water and picnic tables along the banks of the Cass River.

Curtis quickly leads out of Frankenmuth as a newly paved, pot-hole-free road; that wasn't true earlier in the ride. There is little shoulder here or for the next 10 miles but there is also little traffic as you re-enter the country setting. Within a mile Curtis becomes Ormes Road and at *Mile 20.5* you can stand on the edge of the road and enjoy a view of the Cass as it meanders back and forth below you.

The tour departs Ormes at *Mile 21.9*, heads left (north) on Bray Road and left (west) on Van Cleve Road in the hamlet of Tuscola to begin the journey back to Saginaw. There's the Tuscola General Store at the corner if you need a pop or a sugar boost. Van Cleve quickly becomes Tuscola Road and finally the monotonous spell of a flat surface is broken. Tuscola begins with a few dips as it passes rolling farm fields and dairy farms on one side, quick glimpses of the Cass River on the other.

At *Mile 25*, however, it arrives at a spot on the edge of a river bluff where below you are three bends of the Cass River and on the horizon the steeples and clock towers of Frankenmuth. In a flat county, this is a rather surprising view.

In less than 2 miles, you re-enter Little Bavaria, passing Memorial Park and Rose Garden and then arriving at Main Street again at *Mile 26.5*. Here at the corner of Tuscola and Main is a small park with benches, a drinking fountain and the shops of Frankenmuth all around you. Across the street, however, is Frankenmuth Brewery (how convenient!), the award-winning brewers of Frankenmuth and Old Detroit beer. Within the brewery is a gift shop and hospitality room, and brewery tours are offered daily for a small fee. Call the beer maker (☎ 517-652-6183) in advance for the times of the tours.

Stage three (17.4 miles) Continue west of town on Tuscola Road which for the next 2.9 miles is designated a "Natural Beauty Road." You get to cycle most of it along a route that includes a series of gentle hills past more farms, small tracts of woods and views of the Cass River. Still no shoulders here but again traffic is usually very light. You finally depart Tuscola Road at **Mile 29.7** when you turn right (north) on Maple and then at **Mile 32** turn left (west) on Baker Road.

Baker begins the final leg of the ride where you sneak back into the city after a day in the country. At **Mile 32.9** Baker Road makes a short jog south on S. Reimer Road and then resumes heading west. At **Mile 34** you come to a stop sign at Portsmouth Road and then in another mile climb the bypass over I-75 to enter Bridgeport, a bedroom community of Saginaw.

Dixie Highway is reached for the second time at **Mile 36.5** and you cross it carefully to continue on State Street for 20 yards and then turn right on Williamson Road. At State and Williamson is an old iron bridge over the Cass River that has since been converted for foot traffic and turned into a pleasant park strip.

Traffic on Williamson is heavier, but the road has wide gravel shoulders. In less than a mile, you turn left (west) on Washington Avenue and follow it for the next 3 miles. At **Mile 40.6**, or just before Washington becomes a busy road and cyclist's nightmare, you turn left (west) onto Elsie Road.

This quiet residential street will lead you to M-13 almost directly across from Wickes Park Drive, which you then backtrack to end this 43-mile route at the YMCA.

Shorter Option (10 miles) A pleasant shorter option is to begin the ride in Frankenmuth's Heritage Park. Head south on Weiss Road and then west on Curtis Road. The route is the same as described above, only you end back in Frankenmuth in time for a chicken dinner at Zehnder's.

Bicycle sales, service

The Stable, 300 S. Hamilton, Saginaw, 48602; ☎ (517) 799-0601.

Bicycle Village, 5675 Bay, Saginaw, 48604; ☎ (517) 792-8121.

Wesley's Bicycle Shop, 512 W. Genesee, Saginaw; ☎ (517) 752-7501.

Area Attractions

Saginaw Children's Zoo, Saginaw; ☎ (517) 759-1657.

Anderson Water Park, Saginaw; ☎ (517) 759-1386.

Japanese Tea House, Saginaw; ☎ (517) 759-1648.

Shiawassee National Wildlife Refuge, Saginaw; ☎ (517) 777-5930.

Bronner's Christmas Wonderland, Frankenmuth; ☎ (517) 652-9931.

Frankenmuth Brewery, Frankenmuth; ☎ (517) 652-6183.

Frankenmuth Riverboat Tours, Frankenmuth; ☎ (517) 652-8844.

Michigan's Own Military & Space Museum, Frankenmuth; ☎(517) 652-8005.

Area Events And Festivals

May: Skyfest, Frankenmuth.

June: Great Saginaw River Fishing Event, Saginaw; Bavarian Festival, Frankenmuth.

July: Greek Festival, Saginaw.

August: Ethnic Festival, Saginaw.

October: Oktoberfest, Frankenmuth.

Travel information

Tri-City Cyclists, PO Box 2156, Bay City, MI 48707.

Saginaw County Convention and Visitor's Bureau; ☎ (800) 444-9979.

Frankenmuth Convention and Visitor's Bureau; ☎ (800) FUN-TIME.

Cycling Trip Tip #12

To save wear and tear on your brake pads, sit straight up during long descents to use your body as a wind breaker. This alone will slow you down 10 mph.

Downtown Chesaning features many shops, restaurants and a delightful bed and breakfast, making it an ideal place to begin or end a bike tour.

21

Showboat Cruise

Trip Card

Starting Point: Chesaning
County: Saginaw
Distance: 33 miles
Shorter Option: 9.4 miles
Terrain: flat
Highlights: Chesaning, Shiawassee River, country roads
Suggested riders: beginners

Cyclists looking for a tune-up ride early in the season, or a place to go for speed, should try this smooth-sailing route that begins in Chesaning, located southwest of Saginaw.

This route traverses only a few roads, so it's easy to pick up the speed, especially on the ruler-straight South Hemlock Road that runs north and south for 12 miles. Soothing scenes of corn and bean fields, flat country roads and the amenities of St. Charles and Chesaning make this area fun to explore on a bicycle.

Chesaning is best known as Michigan's Showboat City. A musical extravaganza staged on the deck of the Chesaning Showboat in the Shiawassee River has drawn visitors to the town for the past 50 years. The annual event includes a Showboat Parade and headline acts such as Lee Greenwood, Marie Osmond and other country stars.

We also enjoyed strolling through Chesaning's section of antique and collectible shops, which are filled year 'round with Christmas decorations. With shop names like Heavenly Creations, Goody Closet, Truly Scrumptious and Fancy That, this historic area is a great place to find items like porcelain dolls, Amish wooden toys, oak tables, potpourri, tea samples or unique cards. Most of the shop owners live in these historic, early 1900's homes from which they sell their antiques and collectibles.

Stage one (8 miles) We parked behind the Showboat Restaurant in a small lot. In the downtown business district of Chesaning, turn right (north) onto Line Street, a road that makes a few curves and is bumpy at first. You'll cycle through some shady residential areas before the road straightens out and becomes Sharon Road. By **Mile 1.2**, you're out in open country where you'll pass cornfields and a classic, red barn. At **Mile 4.4** turn right (east) onto Marion Road to continue heading north on Sharon Road. This very flat road makes a few curves.

At **Mile 8** you'll pass a residential section of St. Charles and then reach the downtown business district. Within town there are Frank's Supermarket and Tony's (home of the Giant steak sandwich!), along with other places for food. Head to the Field Office of the Shiawassee River State Game Area in the downtown area (just look for the DNR signs) for a pleasant place along the banks of the Bad River to enjoy your lunch.

Nearby is the interesting St. Charles Waterfowl Observatory, which features a pond, flight areas and nesting boxes for a variety of waterfowl and interpretive displays.

Stage two (20.4 miles) Rest up and get plenty of nourishment for this long stage. As you head north out of St. Charles, you will cross the south branch of the Bad River. To leave St. Charles, turn left (north) on Maple, which becomes West Dempsey Road after it winds past the St. Charles public schools. Turn right (north) on Fordney Road at **Mile 11.6** and within a half mile, turn left (west) onto Townline Road.

From Townline Road, another flat road, turn left (south) onto Hemlock Road at **Mile 14**. Hemlock Road is a great one for picking up speed. At **Mile 17.3**, you will reach the tiny town of Brant, where you'll find Nixon's Grocery Store at the corner of South Hemlock and Brant Road.

From Brant, it's possible to make a sidetrip to one of Saginaw County's most scenic spots, Ringwood Forest. To reach the county park turn left (east) on Brant Road for 2 miles and then left (north)

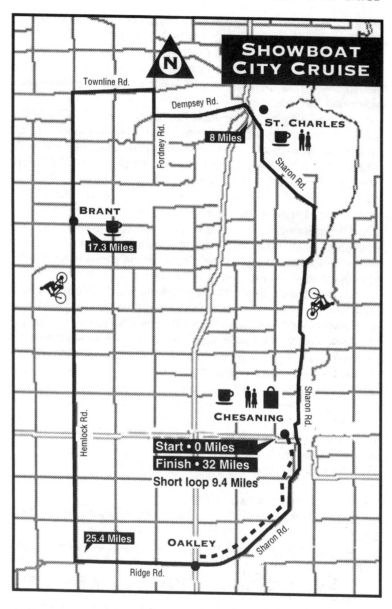

SHOWBOAT CITY CRUISE

Townline Rd.

Dempsey Rd.

Fordney Rd.

8 Miles

ST. CHARLES

Sharon Rd.

BRANT

17.3 Miles

Hemlock Rd.

CHESANING

Start • 0 Miles
Finish • 32 Miles

Short loop 9.4 Miles

Sharon Rd.

25.4 Miles

OAKLEY

Sharon Rd.

Ridge Rd.

on Fordney Road to the park's entrance at the corner of Ring Road and Fordney. Ringwood Forest is split in half by the South Branch of the Bad River and features more than 6 miles of foot trails, a picnic area and a canoe launch. This spot is stunning during fall colors in mid-October. Add 6 miles to your total mileage if you make this side trip.

Heading south on Hemlock Road, you cross M-57 at **Mile 22.4** before turning left (east) onto Ridge Road within a mile. This road takes you through the small, pleasant town of Oakley. At **Mile 28.4** you will need to make a quick left to cross M-52 before turning right onto Sharon Road.

Stage three (4.6 miles) In this last, quick stage, Sharon Road winds its way back to Chesaning, past cemeteries and shaded residential areas. The road narrows somewhat near Chesaning where residents spruce up their yards in the summer with a delightful variety of annuals and perennials.

Sharon Road follows the Shiawassee River high up on a bluff where you can catch glimpses of the flowing water that you would miss from a car. The road becomes Front Street in Chesaning after you pass Showboat Park at **Mile 32.5**. A half mile later turn left (west) onto Broad Street to reach the parking lot behind the Showboat Restaurant at **Mile 33**. Time to go antiquing after you have a chocolate malt at the ice cream parlour behind the restaurant! Yum.

Shorter option (9.4 miles) Cycling from Chesaning south to Oakley and back, via Sharon Road, takes you on a scenic journey along the river for beginners or others wanting a shorter trip.

Bicycle sales, service

Lawson's Bicycle Shop, 511 Brady, Corunna; ☎ (517) 743-5987.

House of Wheels, 814 W. Main St., Owosso; ☎ (517) 725-8373.

Assenmacher Cycling Center, 3526 Davison Rd., Flint; ☎ (810) 635-7844.

Gill-Roy's, 3215 Martin Luther King, Flint; ☎ (810) 787-6581.

Assenmacher Cycling Center, G-1272 W. Hill Rd., Grand Blanc;

☎ (810) 232-2994.

Grand Blanc Cyclery, G-5693 S. Saginaw, Flint; ☎ (810) 694-2811.

Assenmacher Cycling Center, 8053 Miller Road, Swartz Creek; ☎ (810) 635-7844.

The Stable, 300 S. Hamilton, Saginaw; ☎ (517) 799-0601.

Wesley's Bicycle Shop, 512 W. Genesee, Saginaw; ☎ (517) 752-7501.

Bicycle Village, 5675 Bay Rd., Saginaw; ☎ (517) 792-8121.

Area events, festivals

May: May Day Antiques Festival, Chesaning Classic & Antique Car Show, Chesaning.

June: Curwood Festival, Owosso.

July: 4th of July Parade, Corunna; Celebration of the Arts and Garden Summer Festival, Curwood Castle Park, Owosso; Chesaning Showboat, Chesaning.

October: Country Autumn Folk Art Festival, Chesaning.

Area attractions

Shiawassee Historical Village, Corunna; ☎ (517)723-3447.

Shiawassee Arts Center, Owosso; ☎ (517)723-8844.

Curwood Castle, Owosso; ☎ (517)723-8354.

Travel information

Chesaning Chamber of Commerce; ☎ (517) 723-8354.

Shiawassee Area Tourism Council; ☎ (517) 723-5149 or (800) 762-1010.

Tri-City Cyclists, PO Box 2156, Bay City, MI 48707.

Saginaw County Convention & Visitors Bureau, ☎ (517) 752-7164 or 800-444-9979.

The Tri-City Cyclists host a variety of organized bike tours throughout mid-Michigan, including the Liberty Tour that begins in Bay City.

22

Bay Area Tour

Trip Card

Starting point: Bay City
County: Bay
Distance: 38 miles
Shorter option: 11 miles
Terrain: primarily flat
Highlights: Riverwalk and Pier, Saginaw River, Bay City State Park
Suggested riders: beginners to intermediate

Bay City hosts one of the largest Fourth of July fireworks displays in Michigan. The fireworks extravaganza is the highlight of a three-day festival that attracts 350,000 people each year including many touring cyclists who participate in the Tri-City Cyclists' "Liberty Tour".

The Tri-City Cyclists (Saginaw, Bay City, Midland) are one of the larger bike clubs in the state. The club appropriately scheduled their tour for that festival weekend, which hums with numerous activities. This 38-mile route, one of the options of the Liberty Tour (there are also rides of 16 miles, 100 kilometers and 100 miles) was used with permission from bike club leaders.

The community's nerve center during the festival, as well as many other events throughout the year, is the Riverwalk and Pier. This 2-mile asphalt path along the banks of the Saginaw River is where you'll find people bicycling, walking, fishing or simply watching the Great Lakes freighters pass on warm summer days. New in the summer of 1994 is a 1,700-foot-long pedestrian bridge from the Riverwalk across part of the river to the Middlegrounds, a small island in the middle of the narrow river. Benches on the bridge offer peaceful resting spots.

The start of the ride is also near the Bay County Community Center in Veterans Memorial Park. The ride gives you and your companions a chance to enjoy the sights and activities of Bay City as well as the surrounding countryside.

Within 6 miles after you begin this route you'll be rewarded with an area highlight, Bay City State Park and the adjacent 1,800-acre Tobico Marsh State Game Area. Here you can take a break and enjoy the beach and numerous nature and hiking trails.

Bay City is a mecca for antique shoppers with a variety of antique stores, many just east of the river in Bay City's downtown area. The highly rated Bay City Antiques Center, on the corner of Third and Water streets, is home to 100 dealers who display and sell their wares. Tours of old lumber barons' homes are also popular, made easier with $1 brochures from the Bay County Historical Museum.

Roughly a two-hour drive from Detroit, Bay City, with its flat roads, numerous activities and homey, Americana appeal is a fine choice for cyclists.

Stage one (5.8 miles) From the Bay County Community Center head left (north) onto J.F. Kennedy Drive along the Saginaw River. Before you cross under Veterans Bridge you'll cycle by Veterans Memorial Park on your right, complete with a picnic area and lots of parking. The Riverwalk is also to your right along the river. Turn left (west) onto Midland Road in less than a mile, then make a right (north) on the bike path. Stay on the bike path until you connect with Ohio Street. As you make your way out of Bay City, you'll turn right (north) onto Walnut and then left (west) onto East North Union. You'll be travelling through the Westown district, a historic area with plenty of shops and food choices to consider later.

Turn right (north) onto Henry Street, a busy, four-lane road with sidewalks on both sides of the road. Careful as you cross the intersection of Wilder Road and Henry Street just after **Mile 2**. You'll pass a Hot'N Now and a Shell station with a food mart while the largest mall in the area, the Bay City Mall, is one block to your right of this busy corner.

BAY CITY STATE PARK

State Park Rd.

BAY CITY

5.8 Miles

Start • 0 Miles
Finish • 38 Miles
Short loop 11 Miles

Stone Is.

34.4 Miles

Two Mile

Amelith

Three Mile

Beaver Rd.

Mackinaw Rd.

27.8 Miles

Hotchkiss Rd.

N

BAY TOUR

Garfield Rd.

15.1 Miles

19.4 Miles

As you pass the Wilder intersection, Henry Street has paved shoulders on both sides and eventually becomes State Park Drive. The flat road narrows to two lanes as you pick up speed on your way to Bay City State Park. I couldn't help but notice the many rummage sales on the Sunday afternoon we cruised through. If your bike bags are roomy enough, you just may want to stop for some lightweight bargains from these spirited, weekend vendors. There's an access to the Kawkawlin River on your right at **Mile 3.4** followed by a residential section and lots of trees.

You'll pass Captain Jake's Landing, a restaurant with outdoor dining on the Kawkawlin River at **Mile 4.5**. The road curves to the left when it enters Bay City State Park. As you cycle through the park, you'll notice the road, with narrow paved shoulders, is nicely lined with trees. The state park and marsh area are great spots for a break, a good place to camp or a destination to explore after your ride.

There are no fees for cyclists entering the state park reached at **Mile 5.8**. The Jennison Nature Center, open from 10 a.m. to 4 p.m., Wednesday through Sunday, includes spots for bird watching and live wildlife exhibits. The paved Frank Andersen Nature Trail, less than a mile long, links the state park to the Tobico Marsh State Game Area. You can hike a trail system that crisscrosses the state game area or climb a 30-foot tower to observe waterfowl. The entire game area is home to a plethora of birds, waterfowl and other non-humans like deer, beaver, muskrat and mink.

Stage two (13.6 miles) Hopefully, you will be rested for this stage of more than 10 miles. As you make your way out of the park you'll notice the big smiling ice cream cone from the Mussell Beach Drive-in, a place for the cyclist's favorite — ice cream! Continue along Beaver Road, crossing County Road 247 at **Mile 6**, followed by a golf driving range on the right.

Beaver Road is a relatively wide two-lane road through residential and wooded areas. Once the road makes a noticeable curve to your left, it's posted as Beaver Road and from here it's ideal for cycling as it's flat with little traffic. You'll cycle past Two Mile Road, the Parkview General Store and then the Spring Valley Golf Course at **Mile 7.7**. If you need party supplies, you'll laugh at the huge PARTY STORE sign in front of the "76" gas station at **Mile 11.3** just past the busy I-75 and US-23 exchange.

Beyond the intersection is more farmland and a flat straightaway for picking up speed. You'll pass Nine Mile Road at **Mile 14** before turning left (south) onto Garfield Road a mile later. Garfield has gravel shoulders and winds through open country and past a small ma-and-pa party store called Maples Grocery & Party Store at the corner of Wheeler at **Mile 17**. The road is still flat as you pass Wilder and North Union roads before you reach the town of Auburn at **Mile 19.4**.

This town's claim to fame is the Auburn Cornfest, which takes place every summer in July. My local resource for this route said the beer tent is the place to be during this festival.

Stage three (18.6 miles) In Auburn you'll pass a residential section and Auburn Square, a strip mall to your left, and McDonald's and a family restaurant on your right. You'll cross a bridge over US-10 at **Mile 20** and pass Salzburg Road before the road curves to your left (east). Head left (east) onto Hotchkiss Road at **Mile 22**. Hotchkiss is near a county border marked with a "Welcome to Saginaw County" sign. This open road is a little bumpy and has shoulders on both sides.

Before you turn right onto Mackinaw Road at **Mile 27**, you'll cycle by more open country, Eight Mile Road, cross the Seven Mile Road intersection and see a sign for "Frankenlust Township: Heart of the Tri-Cities". Mackinaw Road can be busy at times when nearing Delta Community College, reached at **Mile 27.4**. Turn left (east) into the college and then right (south) onto the two-lane West Campus Road at **Mile 27.8**. You'll cycle by two small dorms on your right and classrooms to your left on this pleasant campus. Within a mile turn left (east) onto Delta Road, which can be busy, especially during mid-week when classes are in session.

You leave the campus on Delta Road and then pass a fire station, a small park with playground equipment and picnic tables and a classic red barn at **Mile 30**. You're now at M-84 and the trickiest intersection of the ride. You want to stay to your right and cross M-84 (also called Bay Road) to reach Three Mile Road on the other side.

Head south on Three-Mile Road, a two-lane road through residential and farm land that can be busy at times. Turn left (east) onto Amelith Road, where the traffic will be considerably lighter. As you make your way over I-75, you'll cycle up one of the few hills on the route at **Mile 31.5**. You can only turn left (north) on narrow Two Mile Road and then as you near the Bay City limits you turn right (east) onto Stone Island Road. You'll cycle by farmland, a small stream, marshy areas and railroad tracks. Turn left (north) onto South Euclid at **Mile 34.4**, a somewhat bumpy, though lightly traveled road.

You'll enter Bay City, once the home of singer Madonna, who lived here for a brief time as a youngster. Her grandmother is still a resident. Turn right (east) on Backus and then left (north) onto Morton Street at **Mile 35.9**. You will cycle by a ballfield and an industrial area before turning right (east) on Salzburg Road at **Mile 36.4**. One of several Grandpa Tony's Restaurants is on Salzburg. "They serve up a mean pizza," locals say. Turn left (north) at the light onto South Wenona Avenue. The Wanigan Eatery, an "awesome" deli know for its corned beef sandwiches and other favorites, is on your right. You'll make several quick turns here: a right on Ivy, a left on Arbor, left on Mundy, then right on Germania to arrive at Main Street. Cross Main Street to the sidewalk on the other side as you make your way back to J.F. Kennedy Drive and the Bay County Community Center at **Mile 38**, home of a large, outdoor community swimming pool.

Before you reach the community center you can stop and enrich yourself with history at the Trombley Centre House, Bay City's first wood house, constructed in 1837 with Greek Revival architecture. The Trombley brothers, Joseph and Mader, were French-American settlers who built the home that is now in the National Register of Historic Places. In 1981, the home was sent down the Saginaw River from its original site on the east bank.

The area around Centre House is where you'll find a Civil War reenactment every fall. Tours of Civil War campsites and crafts make the "River of Time Living History Encampment" an interesting event to check out.

You've finished this 38-mile route. Time to rest up for the big Fourth of July fireworks, go antiquing or hitch a ride from a friendly boat owner after you eat a well deserved meal, of course.

Shorter option (12 miles) The ride from the Bay County Community Center to Bay City State Park, and then backtracking to Bay City is 12 miles.

Bicycle sales, service
Bell's Cycling, 908 N. Euclid, Bay City: ☎ (517) 686-5372.

Jack's Bicycle Shop, 304 Patterson, Bay City; ☎ (517) 684-1735.

Bay Vac Pedal, 805 Columbus, Bay City; ☎ (517) 892-7516.

R.S. Cycling, 2311 Fairview St., Bay City; ☎ (517) 892-8330.

The Stable, 300 S. Hamilton, Saginaw; ☎ (517) 799-0601.

Wesley's Bicycle Shop, 512 W. Genesee, Saginaw; ☎ (517) 752-7501.

Bicycle Village, 5675 Bay, Saginaw; ☎ (517) 792-8121.

Area events, festivals

March: St. Patrick's day Parade, Bay City.

June: Riverside Art Festival/Folk Festival, Wenona Park; Liberty Classic, Antique Wooden Boat Show Veteran's Park; St. Stanislaus Festival; The Bay City River Roar, Bay City.

July: Fourth of July Fireworks Festival, Veteran's and Wenonah parks; Bay Area Tall Ships, Blues Festival, Wenona Park; St. Hyacinth's Festival, Buick Watersports Weekend, Veteran's and Wenonah parks; Auburn Cornfest, Rock & Wheels, Auburn; Munger Potato Festival.

August: Michigan 60's Rock & Roll Reunion, Wenona Park, Bay City.

September: River of Time Encampment, Bay City.

Area attractions

Bay City State Park: ☎ (517) 684-3020.

Bay City Antique Center: ☎ (517) 893-1116.

Travel information

Tri-City Cyclists, PO Box 2156, Bay City, MI 48707.

Bay Area Convention & Visitor's Bureau; ☎ (517) 893-1222 or (800) 424-5114.

Cycling Trip Tip #13

MORE THAN 70 PERCENT of the drag in cycling is caused by wind resistance against your body. That's why serious cyclists wear tight-fitting, stretch material such as Spandex and Lycra shorts and tops. Even wind breakers should not be flapping around.

Cyclists take a break at the Tridge, the only three-way bridge in Michigan and the starting point for the Maple Syrup Ride.

23

Maple Syrup Ride

Trip Card

Starting point: Midland
County: Midland and Isabella
Distance: 64 miles
Shorter option: 16.4 miles
Terrain: Flat, light traffic
Highlights: The Tridge, rail-trail, Chippewa Nature Center and Chippewa and Pine rivers
Suggested Riders: Intermediate

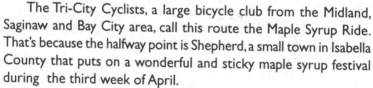

The Tri-City Cyclists, a large bicycle club from the Midland, Saginaw and Bay City area, call this route the Maple Syrup Ride. That's because the halfway point is Shepherd, a small town in Isabella County that puts on a wonderful and sticky maple syrup festival during the third week of April.

But you also could call this ride the River Route. It begins at Midland's Tridge, the only three-way footbridge in the world, or so claim city officials, that is built over the confluence of the Tittabawassee and Chippewa rivers. The first leg of the ride is the perfectly paved Pere Marquette Rail-Trail where you can stop and admire the Tittabawassee River. The second leg parallels the Chippewa River while the third returns from Shepherd along the Pine River.

You end this 64-mile ride by crossing two rivers at once on the Tridge. How appropriate!

For the most part, the Maple Syrup Ride is along flat country roads that have narrow shoulders, if any at all, but also very light traffic. The one exception is the 5.6-mile stretch from Sanford south along Meridian Road. There is far more traffic on this road, especially on Sundays when travelers returning from a weekend up north use it to bypass Midland and a sometimes congested US-10.

If you want to avoid Meridian, begin the ride the way it ends by crossing the Tridge and then heading west on Pine River Road. At Homer Road, head north for a half mile to pick up Chippewa River Road and the rest of the loop to Shepherd.

Midland is an excellent place to begin and end any bike ride. The city has several attractions, including the renowned Dow Gardens, along with a wide range of accommodations and a very pleasant downtown area for shopping. At the Tridge itself a Farmer's Market is held every Saturday throughout the summer, and you can even rent canoes for a paddle on the Tittabawassee just in case riding 64 miles isn't enough exercise for you.

To reach the Tridge, depart US-10 at Business Loop US-10 and follow it into downtown Midland. At Ashman Street, a one-way road, head towards the Tittabawassee River, crossing Main Street and ending at the parking area for the Tridge. There are bathrooms, drinking water and picnic tables in the area.

Stage one (8.2 miles) There is little debate among rail-trail enthusiasts that the Pere Marquette is one of the best de-signed and built rail-trails in Michigan. Someday it will extend for 30 miles from Midland to Clare but today only an 8.2-mile stretch to Sanford is completed and open.

The trail begins at the foot of the Tridge and is marked by a bright red gate with a posted map. In the first mile you ride under-neath M-20, pass fishing docks on the Tittabawassee River and cross the entrance to Emerson Park, another city park on the river. The old cement post near here that reads "Sag 21" is a rail-road marker that indicated the trains were 21 miles from Saginaw.

After passing the Herbert H. Dow Historical Museum and

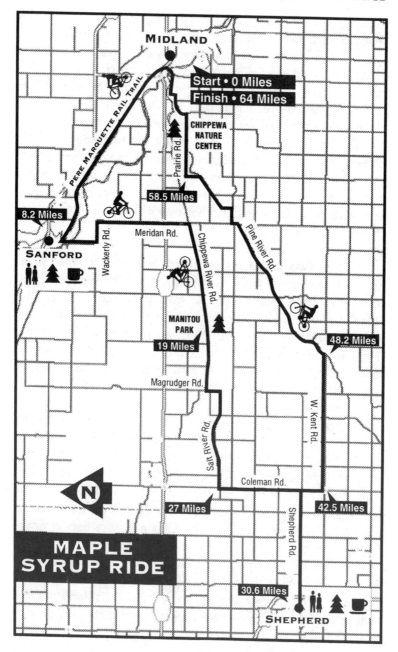

MIDLAND

Start • 0 Miles
Finish • 64 Miles

CHIPPEWA
NATURE
CENTER

PERE MARQUETTE RAIL TRAIL

Prairie Rd.

58.5 Miles

8.2 Miles

SANFORD

Wackerly Rd.

Meridan Rd.

Chippewa River Rd.

Pine River Rd.

MANITOU
PARK

19 Miles

48.2 Miles

Magrudger Rd.

Salt River Rd.

W. Kent Rd.

Coleman Rd.

N

27 Miles

42.5 Miles

Shepherd Rd.

MAPLE
SYRUP RIDE

30.6 Miles

SHEPHERD

crossing Cook Road, the river swings away from the trail. At **Mile 3** you cross Dublin Road and from this point the rail-trail parallels Saginaw Road all the way to Sanford. Saginaw Road can be a busy route but a strip of trees and foliage isolates the trail from most of the traffic and noise. At **Mile 4.8**, you cross Tittabawassee Road and then Pioneer Trail a mile later to skirt the hamlet known as Averill. Here the river returns within view of the rail-trail.

You enter Sanford and at **Mile 8.2** the trail ends at Cedar Street, one block away from Saginaw Road and the heart of Sanford. In town, you'll find a convenience store, an ice cream shop, a restaurant and Sanford Park, where there are picnic tables, bathrooms, drinking water and a pavilion overlooking the Tittabawassee River.

Stage two (10.9 miles) Head west along Saginaw Street to quickly cross the Tittabawassee River. Once over the bridge, immediately turn south (left) on what is posted as Seven Mile Road. Within a third of a mile you pass Cole Road, which leads west to Veterans Memorial Park, get another glimpse of the Tittabawassee River and then ride through two large curves in the next two miles. When the road straightens out at **Mile 10.5**, it's officially Meridian Road and the traffic picks up.

Meridian is well paved and has wide gravel shoulders but it can be busy on Sunday afternoons during the summer. You really only have to endure the heavy traffic for 3 miles until you arrive at Dice Corners at **Mile 13.8**. At this junction, a good deal of the traffic turns onto M-20 while you continue straight on Meridian. There is a large convenience store at Dice Corners (as well as a soft serve ice cream place!) and if you need to stock up on fruit juice or munchies, do it here. There is only one small store between here and Shepherd.

At **Mile 15** you come to a stop sign and turn right on Chippewa River Road. If the traffic has been heavy on Meridian, this road is a sigh of relief. It's newly paved with very narrow shoulders but also light traffic. At **Mile 16**, there's a stop sign at the intersection with Seven Mile Road. Continue on Chippewa River Road as it becomes a predominantly forested avenue.

Need to stretch the legs or see the river again? At **Mile 19**, you arrive at the posted entrance to Manitou Park. Head south (left) along the dirt access road and in a quarter mile you'll reach the Midland County park. This small unit features little more than vault toilets and a parking area. There is no drinking water, but from the parking lot you walk 20 yards through the woods to emerge on a steep bluff overlooking the Chippewa River. It's a scenic spot and there are a couple of picnic tables here in case you feel an urge to break out the munchies.

Stage three (17 miles) From the park entrance, Chippewa River Road continues to head west and after passing the 11 Mile Road intersection, enters a another scenic stretch of forest, much of it part of the Au Sable State Forest. At **Mile 22** you pass a view of the river, and then Chippewa River Road ends at the "T" intersection with Magrudger Road.

Turn south (left) here, cross the Chippewa River and pass Chippewa Valley Canoe Livery and Campground. The route continues as a dirt road beyond the campground and in the next half mile it passes a picturesque log cabin and then makes a wide curve to the west onto Stewart Road. This is a scenic spot. You enter a cool dark forest where flowing past you on the left is the Salt River. Within another half mile the pavement returns and at **Mile 24** you come to the stop sign at the intersection with Alamando Road. Just to the left is an old, one-lane iron bridge crossing Salt Creek with a "50 Ton Limit" (how many candy bars do you have in those saddle bags?). It's a nice place to rest.

The route continues, however, by turning north (right) on Alamando Road and then quickly turning west (left) on Salt River Road. This is another rural road with no shoulders or traffic. It runs right along the river but you never really see it. The tracts of woods, however, are almost as pleasant.

At **Mile 27,** you reach the intersection with Coleman Road where you will find is the one and only party store between Dice Corners and Shepherd. Turn south (left) on Coleman, a no shoulder/no traffic road, that takes you away from the wooded scenery and into the cornfields of the country. You arrive at the intersection with Shepherd Road at **Mile 30.6** where a sign points the way to the town. Turn west (right).

Within a mile you cross the county line between Midland and Isabella counties and then in another 4 miles endure the only incline of the trip - the pedal over US-27. From there it's less than a mile into Shepherd, the *Sweetest Little Town Anywhere Around* the sign proclaims, reached at **Mile 36**. Entering town you pass Little Salt River Park which has picnic tables, bathrooms, drinking water and a pavilion overlooking the river. Practically across the street is an IGA supermarket.

Within Shepherd itself, there is another small park next to the town's historical museum. There are also a couple of restaurants and a bar. The most inviting one is Angel's Subs and Pizza, located in an old movie theater.

Stage four (27.5 miles) The final stage of this ride is a long one with few places to stop and kick off your shoes. Begin by backtracking the 5.5 miles along Shepherd Road to its intersection with Coleman Road. This time head south (right) on Coleman and then at **Mile 42.5** turn east (left) on West Kent Road at a four-way stop intersection.

West Kent begins as a paved road with no shoulders in a rural setting of cornfields and red barns. In August, when I rode it, the corn towered a good six inches over me. Within 3 miles the fields give way to woods as you reenter the Au Sable State Forest and at **Mile 48.2** West Kent ends at a "T" junction with Pine River Road. Turn north (left) on Pine River Road to be immediately greeted with a view of the river.

Pine River Road is another no shoulders/light traffic road. It makes for a very pleasant ride as it winds through a mix of forests and small fields. At **Mile 51.2**, Nine Mile Road intersects into Pine

The Pere Marquette Rail Trail in downtown Midland.

River Road and just south on Nine Mile Road is a bridge over the Pine River.

Within a mile, Pine River Road becomes a newly paved surface with narrow gravel shoulders, and between **Mile 54** and **Mile 55** you enjoy several views of the river. You reach Meridian Road for the second time in another quarter mile; turn north (left) to pass through Gordonville, home of a convenience store and the Gordonville Cafe which offers soft serve ice cream.

Meridian Road can be busy but this time you stay on it only for a quarter mile, turning east (right) on Gordonville Road. At **Mile 56**, you turn north (left) on Pine River Road and follow it as it makes a wide curve past a hay field and then comes to a stop sign at the intersection with 4 1\2 Mile Road. Pine River Road continues northeast here (left) and quickly makes a wide swing where it merges into Homer Road at **Mile 58**. You head north for a half mile and then turn east (right) on Prairie Road, where you pass a sign for Chippewa Nature Center.

After crossing the Pine River at **Mile 60**, the road is again called Pine River Road; and in less than a mile you come to the intersection with Badour Road, where the Chippewa Nature Center is posted again. The nature center, just up Badour, is a wonderful facility. Located where the Chippewa and the Pine Rivers merge, this 1,000-acre nature center includes a 14-mile trail system, an 1870 Homestead Farm and Maple Sugar House and a 16-acre arboretum. The interpretive center itself has a series of interesting displays, a wildlife feeding area and a stunning 60-foot long glass-walled room that overlooks the Pine River.

Pine River Road continues east towards Midland through a wooded area that features the Chippewa Nature Center on one side and Dow Chemical Company land on the other. After winding through a sweeping "S" curve at **Mile 62.5**, you pass Whiting Park's ball fields to the south and then arrive at St. Charles Street which heads north (left) into the other half of the park. St. Charles Street is not posted. Just pedal towards the Tittabawassee River and look for the Whiting Park Overlook at the corner of Sias and Towsley streets, where there is a map and display area. From the overlook you cross the Tridge to end the trip at **Mile 64**. Hungry? Check out Pizza Sam's on Main Street, just up the hill from the Tridge. The eatery has pizza, sandwiches and tables outside.

Shorter Option (16.4 miles) The Pere Marquette Rail-Trail to Sanford and back makes for a 16-mile bike ride that is ideal for families and beginner cyclists not up to a 64-mile route.

Bicycle sales, service

Bryan's Bicycle Shop, 415 E. Main, Midland; ☎ (517) 832-8521.

Motorless Mountain, 121 S. Main, Mt. Pleasant; ☎ (517) 772-2008.

Foltz Bike Shop, 4992 E. Pickard, Mt. Pleasant; ☎ (517) 772-0183.

Ray's Bike Shop, 1000 E. Carpenter, Midland; ☎ (517) 835-1691.

Tri-City Bicycle HQ, 3310 Bay City Rd., Midland; ☎ (517) 496-2810.

Area Attractions

Dow Gardens, Midland; ☎ (517) 631-2677.
H. H. Dow Historical Museum, Midland; ☎ (517) 832-5319.
Dow Visitors Center, Midland; ☎ (517) 636-8658.
Chippewa Nature Center, Midland; ☎ (517) 631-0830.
Chippewa Valley Canoe Livery, Midland; ☎ (517) 835-5657.

Area Events And Festivals

April: Maple Syrup Festival, Shepherd.
May: Highland Festival and Games, Alma.
June: Matrix Festival; Michigan Antique Festival, Midland.
July: Riverdays Festival; Michigan Antique Festival, Midland.
August: Midland County Fair, Midland.

Travel information

Midland County Convention and Visitors Bureau, ☎ (800) 678-1961 or (517) 839-9901.

Tri-City Cyclists, PO Box 2156, Bay City, MI 48707.

Cycling Trip Tip #14

If your posterior is soar after a long ride, invest in a gel seat for your bicycle. It's a an investment, to be sure, but it conforms to the curve of your body and should prevent "saddle soars" the next day. What price is that worth?

Roadside wildflowers are part of any ride in Northeast Michgian through spring and early summer.

Northeast Michigan

Awesome AuSable
Tawas Baywatch
Natural Gaylord
Thunder Bay
Black Lake Tour
Mackinaw Shoreline
Magical Mackinac

Lumbermen's Monument, one of the stops along the AuSable River bike route in the Huron National Forest.

Awesome AuSable

Trip Card

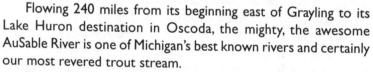

Starting point: Oscoda
County: Iosco
Distance: 47.5 miles
Terrain: some rolling hills
Highlights: AuSable River, Iargo Springs, Canoe Race Monument, Lumberman's Monument
Suggested riders: intermediate

Flowing 240 miles from its beginning east of Grayling to its Lake Huron destination in Oscoda, the mighty, the awesome AuSable River is one of Michigan's best known rivers and certainly our most revered trout stream.

The AuSable's widest points are just west of Oscoda, offering a good cycling route beginning in Oscoda. Roads around the AuSable are perched high above the river on either side. It's not a route for fast cruising as there are many places to stop and enjoy the take-your-breath-away scenery, especially dazzling in the fall.

The Lumbermen's Monument Auto Tour, which circles the area in the Huron National Forest, is a National Scenic Byway as designated by the U.S. Forest Service. The auto route showcases an array of attractions and scenic lookouts. This cycling route is a shortened version of the motorized tour.

History and scenery best sum up what you'll see when cycling this route. Naturally, taking center stage is the AuSable, a river Native Americans, trappers and loggers used for transportation.

Today the river provides electrical power and unparalleled recreation. River Road can be a busy one, especially during the fall color tour season, but its paved shoulders keep cyclists and motorists separate and the ride is well worth putting up with the extra traffic. Schedule time for several breaks to inhale the beauty of the panoramic vistas. The two most notable highlights, less than halfway through the route, are the Lumbermen's Monument, a tribute to the pioneer spirit of Michigan lumbermen, and the soothing waters of the largo Springs (unfortunately, you can't cycle down the 220 steps leading to the springs!)

Stage one (9.2 miles) From US-23 in downtown Oscoda, cycle left on River Road, first heading north before the road turns west. As you head out of town there is are a combination of cement and gravel shoulders before you reach the East Gate Welcome Center, part of the Huron National Forest (an alternate starting point for this route). There's a canoe launch on the AuSable at **Mile 3.9**. As you make your way into the national forest, there's a mixture of pines and hardwoods, especially colorful in the fall. Turn right (north) at **Mile 7** to reach a scenic overlook with tall trees and ferns. Turn right (west), back onto River Road, past an area of cottages, Desi's Family Dining on the right, and the Dam Store (offering bait, tackle and clothing). The Foot Dam (**Mile 8** on your right), built in 1917, is one of six power dams built by the Consumers Power Company on the AuSable River that still generates electrical power. Soon you'll be at the Foot Site Park where there are bathrooms (yea!), a small pavilion, picnic tables, play equipment and even a small gift shop. The AuSable River Queen is also docked here. The paddlewheel river boat offers a two-hour round trip on the AuSable River; something to consider for later.

Stage two (12.3 miles) Within a mile you'll cycle by Old Orchard Park, a lovely spot on the river with campsites and a store. There's a gradual uphill run that crests at **Mile 11**. Though the road narrows near Wilber Road, there are gravel shoulders.

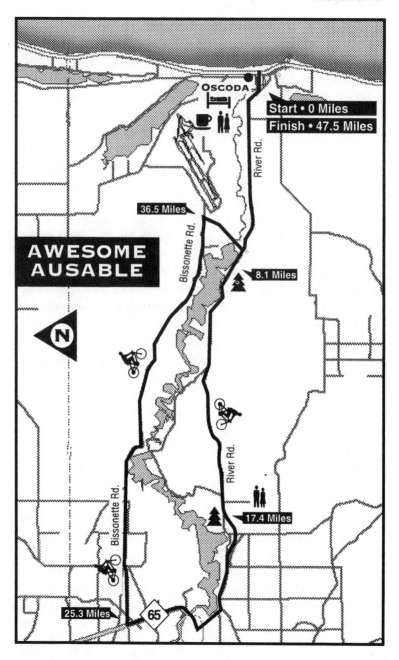

OSCODA

Start • 0 Miles
Finish • 47.5 Miles

River Rd.

36.5 Miles

Bissonette Rd.

8.1 Miles

AWESOME
AUSABLE

N

River Rd.

17.4 Miles

Bissonette Rd.

25.3 Miles

65

This intersection is followed by more gradual hills and a pine plantation near **Mile 14**. After you pass Kobs Road, River Road continues to wind and is a bit bumpy in spots. You pass a resort and campground at **Mile 16.3** followed by a dense forested area. Cycle another mile and turn right (north) on the gravel road to the Lumbermen's Monument stairway. Plan to spend some time here to see one of the most impressive attractions in the area.

A 14-foot bronze statue of a sawyer, a river driver and a timber cruiser with the tools of their lumbering trade dominates the Monument's grounds. The bigger-than-life casting, perched high on a bluff overlooking the beautiful AuSable River, was erected in 1931 at a cost of $50,000, paid for by contributions from the descendants of the lumbermen who harvested Michigan's timber crop. The major industry of the area in the late 1800's and early 1900's comes alive through other lumbering artifacts at the interpretive area and museum. Lumbermen's Monument vividly reminds us of an era in Michigan's history when loggers fought the elements and stripped the land to build this nation.

While you're enjoying the scenery at Lumbermen's Monument, take some prize-winning photos with the backdrop of the Ausable River. You might even spot a deer drinking at the edge of Deer Island that extends from the bay to the main stream. You can also descends the stairs leading to the water's edge where small springs bubble and flow into the river. On the afternoon my friends and I visited the area, we were taken in by the tranquility of the region and the fresh crisp air. At Lumberman's Monument, there are also tables and grills for picnics, modern restrooms in the information center and campsites.

Shortly after you return to River Road (turn right) you'll pass the main entrance to Lumbermen's Monument on Monument Road. Within 1.5 miles you'll cycle by the AuSable River Canoe Monument, a white stone structure dedicated to all past, present and future paddlers who compete in the grueling annual 120-mile Canoe Marathon on the AuSable River, cited as one of this nation's toughest. As an added bonus, you just might site an eagle or two as there is a nest in the area that can be seen from the overlook.

One more main stop west of the canoe monument is the largo Springs Interpretive Site at **Mile 21.5.** At first glance the area looks unimpressive. But lock up the bikes and walk the more than 200 steps down to the river level and you'll understand why the Chippewa Indians considered this a holy place. True to its Indian name (meaning *many waters*), largo Springs is comprised of several springs that spill from the pressure banks under a canopy of towering pine trees and moss covered bluffs.

Stage three (13.5 miles) Shortly after turning right (west) back onto River Road, you will need to turn right (north) onto Highway 65.

You will go down a hill and over a bumpy section of the road before it curves to your left. You'll cross a two-lane iron bridge overlooking the Five Channels Dam on your left at **Mile 23.2,** followed by another bait shop. You'll pass a section of resorts and cabins and cross a dirt road (good for mountain biking) before reaching Bissonette Road at **Mile 25.3,** where you turn right (east). The road here can be busy at times with truck traffic, although it was manageable when we traveled it. The road has asphalt shoulders at first, followed by gravel and grassy shoulders and then no shoulders at all at **Mile 26.8.** The Iosco County Road Commission repaved part of Bissonette from M-65 to Lorenz Road, but Bissonette Road between Lorenz Road and Wilber is a bit rough, with some gravel sections. Bissonette is slated to be resurfaced.

Bissonette Road twists and dips as you cycle by old cottages and residential areas. If in need of a break or refreshments, Anne's Country Store is reached at **Mile 35.**

Stage four (12.5 miles) Roughly 1.5 miles east of the store, turn right (south) on Rea, a narrow road with gravel shoulders that crosses a bridge over the AuSable at **Mile 40.5.** Turn left (east) onto River Road by the Dam Store and backtrack to downtown Oscoda where there's an array of food choices (typical stuff like McDonalds, Arby's, Burger King and Subway), and a bike shop if you're in need of repairs. Local residents recommend Charbonneau's Restaurant with a seafood buffet on weekends, located west of the AuSable River bridge off US-23. Another favorite is Big Dave's Pizza at 5226 N. US-23, an award-winning restaurant that serves up classic crust, pan and deep dish pizza.

Bicycle sales, service
The Bike Shop, 251 S. State St. (US-23), Oscoda, ☎ (517) 739-2639.

Area events and festivals
May: Woodcarvers Show, Oscoda.
June: Art on the Beach, Oscoda Township Beach Park, Oscoda.
July: AuSable River Canoe Marathon, Summer AuSable River Days, Paul Bunyan Festival, Zogdawah Pow-wow, Oscoda.
September: Antique Car Show, Oscoda.

Area attractions
Lumbermen's Monument Visitor Center, Huron National Forest; ☎ (517) 362-4477.

River Road Scenic Byway, Huron National Forest; ☎ (517) 362-4477.

AuSable River Queen; ☎ (517) 739-7351 or (517) 728-5713.
Kiwanis Monument; ☎ (517) 362-4477.

Travel information
Oscoda-AuSable Chamber of Commerce, ☎ (800) 235-4625 or (517) 739-7322.

Cycling Trip Tip #15

Faced with a steep climb along your route? Avoid eating anything heavy 20 or 30 minutes before such an ascent as it won't digest in time for a sugar boost. What is more likely to result is a stomach cramp halfway up the hill.

⟨25⟩

Tawas Baywatch

Trip Card

Starting point: East Tawas
County: Iosco
Distance: 30.6 miles
Shorter option: 11.8 miles
Terrain: mostly flat
Highlights: Tawas Point State Park, East Tawas, Huron National Forest
Suggested riders: beginners to intermediate

When cycling through Tawas City and East Tawas, it was easy for me to understand the popularity of the Tawas area. Sometimes called the Cape Cod of the Midwest, the twin tourist towns offer plenty of shops for browsing, restaurants for dining, parks for strolling, a paved walkway for cycling and nearby natural areas for a variety of outdoor activities.

Sheltered Tawas Bay, actually a bay within a bay, defines and half circles the area, ending in a strip of land at Tawas Point and Tawas Point State Park, your starting point for this 30.6-mile route. With Saginaw Bay to the south and Lake Huron to the east, the Tawas area has long lured residents of Saginaw, Bay City, Midland, Flint and the metro areas of Detroit, Ann Arbor and Toledo. The pristine woods of the Huron National Forest, the scenic inland lakes, rivers and streams and fairly flat, paved roads make the area a natural respite for cyclists and outdoor enthusiasts. There are furnished, small cottages on the bay to rent and ample art shows and festivals are planned each year. In addition, there's camping at the state park.

The Tawases welcome cyclists on a paved walkway/bicycle path, dedicated on Memorial Day in 1992. The path, which extends from the city limits of Tawas City through the city limits of East Tawas, will likely be expanded in the future, according to city officials. All this scenery and all these amenities add up to a fine destination for you, your bicycle and even your non-cycling companions.

Although the area can get crowded with visitors, the ambiance is relaxing and no one's in a big hurry. Best of all, the prices are cheaper than more developed tourist areas on Lake Michigan.

Stage one (5.9 miles) This route begins at the Tawas Point State Park, a popular park with 185 acres and 210 camp sites. You'll want to explore the park's beautiful beach, its classic lighthouse and nature trails at some point during your visit. The Sandy Hook Nature Trail at Tawas Point State Park comes alive with birds during peak migration periods in the spring and fall. Check with the park's contact station for a birding check list. The historic lighthouse, owned and operated by the U.S. Coast Guard, was built at its present location in 1876 and proudly stands at 70 feet above the waters of Tawas Bay.

As you cycle out of the park on Tawas Beach Point Road, there are volleyball courts to your left. Past the entrance of the state park, the shaded road twists and curves and a marina will appear on your left near **Mile 1**. The road forms an arc as you wind around Tawas Bay. There's a 40 mph speed limit here for cars, so be careful, although the road is not usually heavily traveled. You'll cycle past tree-lined sections of hardwoods and evergreens where you'll likely notice other cyclists traveling to and from the park.

At **Mile 2** there are paved asphalt shoulders on both sides of the road, although the road isn't very wide. The road soon curves to your left past a long section of trees and upscale homes on your left. At the stop sign, turn left onto US-23, a very busy inter-

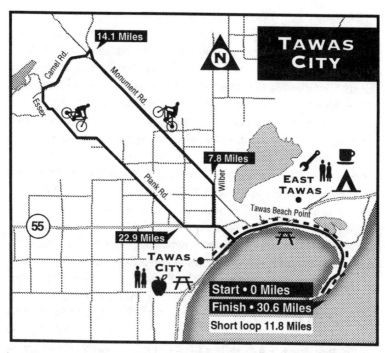

section, especially on holiday weekends. There are sidewalks on the left, part of the paved walkway/bicycle path, and sidewalks on the far right side of the railroad tracks. As you cycle your way into East Tawas and Tawas City, there are lodging choices galore - motels of varying sizes including the Holiday Inn and small cabins. You'll pass municipal parking on the right, an alternative place to begin this route, before riding by the main business district in East Tawas to your right. The business district is a two-block strip with many shops for gifts and souvenirs. There's also a campground to your left at **Mile 4.4**.

Shortly beyond the campground, you'll come upon the scenic East Tawas City Park (☎ 517-362-5562). The park edges up to Tawas Bay, a Michigan State Harbor of Refuge. The park has 170 modern campsites, a sandy beach, a small gazebo, picnic area and restrooms. Past the park there are some eating choices - Kentucky Fried Chicken and Genii's Fine Foods (☎ 517-362-5913), a rustic, family restaurant known for its "really good perch." There are sidewalks on both sides of the road as you reach the city limits of Tawas City. This nice section of the road parallels the water.

To pick up more information on the area, you can visit the Tawas Chamber of Commerce, located on your left at **Mile 5.3**.

Within less than a mile, you'll reach the Tawas City Park, a park with a large, well-built wooden gazebo, picnic tables, a sandy beach, restrooms, a children's play area and a concession stand. The park is an ideal location for your non-cycling friends and family to wait or a great place to take a break and walk on the dock by the bay. Be forewarned! On the rest of the route there are few places to stop for food. So eat now in the Tawases or load up your bike bags with selections from local businesses like the Carter IGA. Between the two towns there are a McDonald's, a Little Caesar's, a Pizza Hut, a Subway and a Dairy Queen as well as local pizzerias and restaurants. G's Pizzeria & Deli in East Tawas (☎ 517-362-8659) is a popular spot for Mexican food and delicious Chef's salad.

Stage two (8.2 miles) From US-23 north of the park, cycle west on Hemlock Road (also called M-55). Although this highway can be busy, there are shoulders on both sides of the road. Cross the Tawas River before turning right onto Wilber Road at **Mile 6.8**. Wilber is a flat, two-lane road with paved shoulders on both sides. After a mile Wilber Road is intersected by Monument Road. Ride left onto Monument. You'll pass a residential section and tree-lined sections on this primarily flat road, which enters into a southern segment of the Huron National Forest.

At **Mile 8.9**, you'll cycle by Charlie's on the Green Restaurant and Golf Course before encountering a section of slightly rolling hills, a residential area and then a stand of pine trees. Monument Road makes a couple of curves before you reach Camel Road.

Stage three: (10.6 miles) Camel Road, somewhat bumpy, has gravel shoulders on both sides and some rolling hills. At **Mile**

14.4, the road rounds a sharp corner and makes a couple of more curves. The road will go up and down before you turn left on Essex Road at **Mile 16.3**. This road is also a bit bumpy at the beginning but eventually smooths out. Turn left onto Plank Road, which is unmarked, at **Mile 17**. This two-lane road has a mixture of grassy and gravel shoulders. Plank Road is also flat and curves through tree-lined stretches before you arrive at a nice straightaway in beginning the return to the Tawases. There's an enjoyable, long gradual downhill beginning at **Mile 19.4** before you go uphill, naturally, past Rempert Road, through a pleasant area of open country. You will pass Kobs Road and then Dean Road at **Mile 22.1**.

Turn left onto M-55 at **Mile 22.9**. This road can be busy, although there are paved shoulders on both sides. You'll pass Tawas Area High School on your right, another possible starting point, before you reach the Tawas City city limits and the intersection of

---

Cycling Trip Tip #16

THERE'S NOTHING WORSE THEN TAKING A SWIG FROM YOUR WATER BOTTLE AND TASTING THE FRUIT JUICE YOU HAD IN THERE FROM THE BICYCLE TRIP BEFORE. FACE IT, A PLASTIC bottle absorbs the taste and smell of whatever you last put in there.

There are several ways to eliminate the lingering taste of juices from one tour to the next. Baking soda, which you put in your refrigerator to absorb smells, will also work in your bottle if you rinse it out with warm water and a teaspoon of baking soda. Or let the bottle stand overnight filled with water and a tablespoon of lemon juice. Or, heavens forbid, just wash your water bottle immediately after a tour. That in itself will eliminate the taste of most liquids.

Hemlock Road and Lake Street by Tawas Bay at **Mile 24.7**.

Stage four (5.9 miles) Now's the time to either head back to the state park, to browse in the Tawas shops or linger at one of the city parks or restaurants. Outdoor enthusiasts will thoroughly enjoy a visit to Nordic Sports at 218 W. Bay, in East Tawas, a place for outdoor clothing, books on a variety of topics, cross country skis and trail maps, binoculars, bicycles, bike helmets, kayaks, camping gear and all that other fun stuff nature lovers drool over!

Backtrack on US-23 before turning right onto Tawas Beach Point Road which will take you to Tawas Point State Park. Time to stretch those legs, take a walk on the nature trails or just relax by the campsite.

Shorter option (11.8 miles) Cycling from the state park to the Tawas City Park, via Tawas Beach Point Road and US-23 makes for a leisurely ride for beginners, especially those who want to shop or watch the people and the boats on Tawas Bay. After reaching the City Park, backtrack to the state park.

Bicycle sales, service
Nordic Sports, 218 W. Bay St., East Tawas; ☎ (517) 362-2001.

Area events and festivals
May: spring bird migration.

June: Tawas Point Celebration Days, Tawas Bay Lake Trout Super Tournament, East Tawas Downtown Arts and Crafts Show.

July: Independence Day Parade and Fireworks, Tawas area; MarinerFest, Tawas area.

August: Tawas Bay Waterfront Fine Arts Show; Grant Township Summer Festival; Sidewalk Sale Days, Jazz Festival.

September: Labor Day Weekend Arts & Crafts Show.

October: Oktoberfest, Tawas Bay.

Travel information
Tawas Area Chamber of Commerce, Tawas Bay Tourist and Convention Bureau, ☎ (800)55-TAWAS.

Tawas Point State Park: ☎ (517) 362-5041.

26

Natural Gaylord

Trip Card

Starting point: downtown Gaylord
Distance: 28.4 miles
County: Otsego
Terrain: very hilly
Highlights: woods, steep hills, Gaylord,
Coca Cola Museum
Suggested riders: advance

An elk herd. Championship golf greens. Four seasons of recreation. The Alpine Village of northern Michigan. These are your clues. Give up?

You're right if you guessed Gaylord, strategically located in the top half of the Lower Peninsula. Gaylord's popularity has boomed with the development of more than 20 golf courses and inviting resorts with all the amenities. Because of the area's terrain and its close proximity to many other prime cycling spots, Gaylord is a great destination for bicyclists as well.

But if you're looking for a leisurely route with flat roads, skip this one. It's hilly. Although not all that long at 28.4 miles, and not totally an endless series of hills, this route does feature some of the biggest hills on any trip in this book. If you and your cycling companions want a conditioning ride to see if those granny gears are working, this is the route for you.

The route takes you past resorts, over the Sturgeon River and up, up, up many hills as well as through some beautiful wooded areas. You can even make a stop at The Bottle Cap Museum and Gift Shop, a Coca Cola memorabilia collection where the owner gives out free Coke with museum tours.

Every July for more than 30 years Gaylord pays homage to its heritage and moves into full Swiss mode for the annual Alpenfest. Main Street becomes Alpenstrasse as the location of many festival events. The week long festival includes traditions like the Boogg, a huge paper mache effigy that is set afire to consume the troubles of those who come to join the fun. There's a Queen's Pageant, a free pancake and sausage breakfast, foot races and the Alpenfest Grand Parade and Swiss Olympics.

This route begins on M-32 in Gaylord, reached by departing I-75 at exit 282 and heading east.

Stage one (9.5 miles) There's parallel parking in the downtown area of Gaylord on M-32, called Main Street in town. Downtown Gaylord is home to many shops and restaurants including the The Alphorn Shop, Seven Oaks Outfitters, a place with outdoor gear. Head east on M-32, which can be busy, to quickly depart town. M-32 has five lanes at first and sidewalks on both sides.

Within the first mile you'll pass the expansive Hidden Valley Resort. The road goes downhill with paved shoulders on both sides. By **Mile 2.5** you know you're "up north" with plenty of tall hardwoods trees lining the road. You'll travel up a long, gradual uphill (you haven't seen anything yet!) where there are valleys, fields and trees to your left at **Mile 3.2**. The Big Lake Party Store will be on your left, followed by a Big Lake public access on your right at **Mile 4.4**.

The route continues along a gradual downhill and then uphill before M-32 makes a sharp curve to the south. Don't follow the curve, continue straight on Beckett Road and then make a left (north) on Turtle Lake Road at **Mile 6.5**. Turtle Lake Road is a narrow country road with cows, barns and wooded stretches. Make a quick left (west) on Wilkinson Road at **Mile 7.3** then an immediate right (north) on Dover Road, a pretty road with gravel shoulders. You make your way up a hill and are rewarded from the top with a nice view of the rolling hills ahead.

A couple of fun downhill sections begin at **Mile 7.7** where the trees are so close at times you can almost touch them from your bike. On a mountain bicycle you could continue straight ahead at **Mile 8.5** as the road turns to dirt. But for this road route, turn

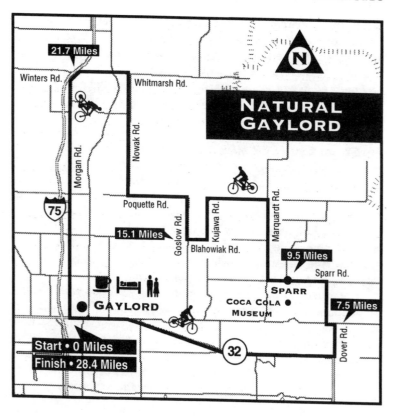

Natural Gaylord

21.7 Miles

Winters Rd.

Whitmarsh Rd.

Morgan Rd.

Nowak Rd.

75

Poquette Rd.

Goslow Rd.

Kujawa Rd.

Marquardt Rd.

15.1 Miles

Blahowiak Rd.

9.5 Miles

Sparr Rd.

7.5 Miles

SPARR

COCA COLA MUSEUM

GAYLORD

Dover Rd.

Start • 0 Miles

Finish • 28.4 Miles

32

left (west) on Sparr Road at **Mile 8.5**. Initially you'll go uphill on this road and will certainly enjoy the open field where you can see off into the distance before the hill crests within a third of a mile.

At **Mile 9.5** you've reach the small burg of Sparr, little more than an intersection with a gas station. Just past Whitehouse Trail is the The Bottle Cap Museum and Gift Shop, a museum filled with 3,000 items of Coca Cola memorabilia. Owners Bill and Ethel Hicks dispense free Coca Cola with a museum tour which costs $2.50 for adults and $1.50 for children. Museum hours are 11 a.m. to 5 p.m. on Wednesday, Thursday, Friday and Saturday.

Back in 1976 Hicks uncovered several white Coca Cola bottles which led to a hobby of collecting Coca Cola memorabilia. A vast array of Coca Cola stuff fills two floors: pencils, erasers, openers pencil cases, matchbooks, checkers, a wall mural, Coke bottles, Coca Cola coolers and a Santa poster to name a few. The collectibles are housed in cabinets, hang from the ceiling and sit on the floor - there are even two Coca-Cola bicycles with the renowned red & white trademark. The museum may be a nice spot to look around and rest a bit. Coca Cola memorabilia are for sale in the museum's gift shop.

Stage two (11.2 miles) Past the museum Sparr Road narrows and goes through a nice wooded section. Turn right (north) on Marquardt Road at **Mile 10**. One of those big hills I've been telling you about begins within a half mile and doesn't crest until **Mile 10.8**. This is followed by more hills. The shoulders on Marquardt Road are bumpy but the road is lightly traveled. You'll cycle by some apple trees before you make a left (west) on Seymore Road at **Mile 12**. After you climb another big hill you reach a nice vantage point at **Mile 12.4**, gazing upon very hilly terrain.

Breathe deeply as you reach another hilly section where you'll pass another stand of trees close enough to touch. More hills. The road makes a 90-degree curve to your left and becomes Kujawa Road, then curves to your right on a newly paved section.

Cycle to your right (north) on Goslow Road at **Mile 15** where you'll get to travel up yet another hill. At **Mile 16**, turn left (west) on Poquette Road, a road with bumpy shoulders. This route continues with a downhill stretch and then a very steep uphill that crests in a half mile. But don't worry as you look ahead, you don't have to travel up the entire hill.

Turn right (north) on Nowak Road at **Mile 17.7**, which makes a curve through yet more hills. The road does level out a bit near **Mile 19** only to be followed by more hills, although not quite as steep as the last ones. Turn left (west) on Whitmarsh Road at **Mile 20.7** and you'll make a sharp curve before reaching an odd intersection at Whitmarsh, Winters and Old US-27. Stop and take a breath, the biggest hill is yet to come.

Stage three (7.7 miles) Whitmarsh Road becomes Winters Road after you cross over Old US-27 and then cruves to the right as a road with gravel shoulders. Winters Road makes a couple more sharp curves before you make a left (south) on Morgan

One of the highlights of the Gaylord tour is a stop at the Bottle Cap Museum and Gift Shop. (Photo by Dennis Powell)

Road at **Mile 21.7**. A quarter-mile climb begins at **Mile 22.5** and is followed by - Yikes!- the steepest uphill yet. Those of you lucky enough to have granny gears can climb it but others might have to push their bikes up this one.

The road levels out past a horse farm at **Mile 24**. You pass a large cemetery and then reach Gaylord at **Mile 26.7**. There are a couple of four-way stops signs before you reach M-32. At **Mile 27.8** the La Seniorita Restaurant is straight ahead and Burger King is to your right. Turn left and use caution at this busy corner as you journey back to downtown Gaylord.

Hungry? You'll also pass Arby's, TCBY Yogurt, Kentucky Fried Chicken, Subway and the highly reccommended Sugar Bowl Restaurant for deli sandwiches or homemade soup before you reach the starting point of this route in front of the Alphorn Shop. Congratulations on conquering those hills!

Bicycle sales, service

Alphorn Sports Shop, 137 W. Main, Gaylord; ☎ (517) 732-5616.

Banhof Sports, 128 W. Main, Gaylord; ☎ (517) 732-9421.
Wheels 'N Motion, 110 Otsego, Gaylord; ☎ (517) 732-6989.
The Bicycle Shop, 200 E. Michigan, Grayling; ☎ (517) 821-6559.

Area attractions

Pigeon River Country State Forest , Vanderbilt; ☎ (517) 983-4101.

Call of the Wild Museum, Gaylord; ☎ (800) 835-4347.
Otsego County Historical Museum; ☎ (517) 732-6662.
The Bottle Cap Museum, Sparr; ☎ (517) 732-1931.

Area events and festivals

May: Memorial Day Parade & Concert, Gaylord; Morel Mushroom Festival, Lewiston.

June: Gus Macker Basketball Tournament, Gaylord; Mancelona Bass Festival, Mancelona; Jordan Valley Freedom Festival, East Jordan.

July: Alpenfest, Gaylord.

August: Otsego County Fair, Michaywe' Arts and Craft Fair, Snowmobile Grass Drag Race, Gaylord; Outdoor Art Fest, Lewiston.

Travel information

Gaylord/Otsego County Chamber of Commerce, ☎ (517) 732-4000.

Gaylord Area Convention & Tourism Bureau, ☎ (800) 345-8621.

Cycling Trip Tip #17

How many calories do you burn while biking? A 135-pound person riding at 15 mph burns close to 11 calories per minute. For every additional 15 pounds above that you add another 1.2 calories per minute. Roughly 3,500 calories equals one pound of body weight so a 150-pound person would need to cycle almost five hours to burn off a pound.

27

Thunder Bay

Trip Card

Starting point: Alpena
County: Alpena, Presque Isle
Distance: 35 miles
Shorter Option: 7 miles
Terrain: flat to rolling hills
Highlights: Alpena, Long Lake, Seven Mile Pond
Suggested riders: intermediate

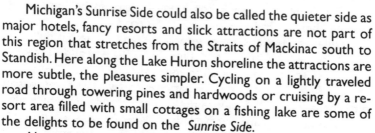

Michigan's Sunrise Side could also be called the quieter side as major hotels, fancy resorts and slick attractions are not part of this region that stretches from the Straits of Mackinac south to Standish. Here along the Lake Huron shoreline the attractions are more subtle, the pleasures simpler. Cycling on a lightly traveled road through towering pines and hardwoods or cruising by a resort area filled with small cottages on a fishing lake are some of the delights to be found on the *Sunrise Side*.

Alpena, with a population of 12,000 and the starting point for this route, is the only real city in the region. Sheltered by Thunder Bay, Alpena has a rich and colorful history of lumbering, limestone and shipwrecks. With a huge supply of limestone, Alpena emerged as a "Cement City" in the 19th century and today the Besser Manufacturing Company is still the world leader in concrete block-making equipment.

The historic downtown area known as Old Town Alpena features small and specialized shops including The Country Cupboard in the old Sepull's Pharmacy, a landmark in Alpena, located at 102 North Second Street.

This cycling route runs northeast of Alpena before turning west along Long Lake and looping back to town past views of Seven Mile Pond that flows into the Thunder Bay River. The route features lightly traveled roads and plenty of woods for a relaxing, soothing jaunt in northern Michigan. For a shorter option around Alpena, be among the first to cycle the town's new River Path (construction completed in 1995) following the Thunder Bay River where you can stop at Island Park and other natural areas of Alpena.

Stage one (10.3 miles) There are several beaches and small parks along Thunder Bay in Alpena including Starlight Beach, Blair Park, Thompson Park and Bay View Park, as well as a couple of public boat launches. Alpena's main swimming area is located at Mich-e-ke-wis Park on the south end of the city limits just off US-23. We parked in the City of Alpena's marina parking lot near the downtown area near the 90-degree curve of US-23. From Prentiss Street, return to US-23 (also called State Avenue here) and make a left to continue to follow the state highway through downtown Alpena. Here US-23 becomes Chisholm Street but just keep following the state highway signs.

The heart of Alpena's commercial area can be busy. After passing Nathan's Family Restaurant, the road widens as you cycle by residences, businesses, governmental and industrial buildings. You'll also pass a Wendy's, a McDonald's, a Big Boy and a local deli - all places to consider for after your ride.

At **Mile 2.7** the road narrows to two lanes and passes the Alpena Flying Club before the scenery changes to a nice mixture of evergreens and hardwoods at **Mile 7**. Cycle left on Long Lake Road by the Long Lake Chapel at **Mile 7.4,** a forested road that's a bit bumpy in spots. The road closely hugs Long Lake and at **Mile 9.6** there's a small store at the water's edge. A sprinkling of cottages and birch trees let you know you're "up north." The Long Lake Supermarket is on your left at **Mile 10.3**. Maybe it's time for some juice or a chocolate bar.

Stage two (15.3 miles) Continue by turning left on Long Lake Road, which has gravel shoulders but lightly traveled. You enter Presque Isle County at **Mile 13** where there are some rolling hills straight ahead. The road then twists and turns, providing

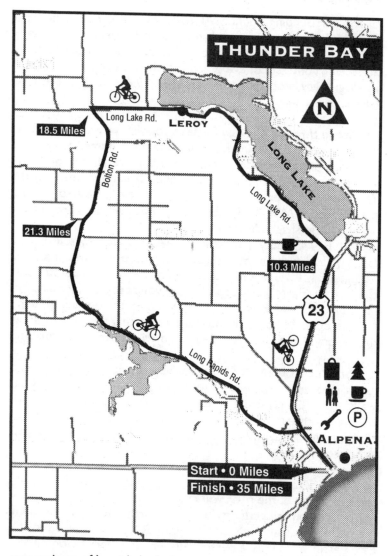

THUNDER BAY

18.5 Miles

Long Lake Rd.

LEROY

Bolton Rd.

LONG LAKE

Long Lake Rd.

21.3 Miles

10.3 Miles

23

Long Rapids Rd.

ALPENA

Start • 0 Miles
Finish • 35 Miles

many views of Long Lake before you cycle up a large hill and turn left (south) on Bolton Road at *Mile 18.5*.

On this road there's a mixture of open country, farms and trees lining the road. Just past the "Welcome to Maple Ridge Township" sign there's a fun downhill stretch that also provides a view of the surrounding country. At **Mile 21.3** you reach the small burg of Bolton, little more than a railroad crossing, a couple of homes, an abandoned store and the Bolton Bar. Past Bolton there are scenic contrasts of evergreens, hardwoods and open fields. A small grocery store is passed at **Mile 25.6** and then the road curves to the left.

Stage three (9.4 miles) Cycle to your left where Bolton Road merges into Long Rapids Road at **Mile 25.7**. Immediately, there are wide, paved shoulders and a beautiful stretch of woods followed by glimpses of Seven Mile Pond, an impoundment of the Thunder Bay River. The road is a bit bumpy before you pass a party store at **Mile 28.5**, followed by more watery views of the jigsaw puzzle-shaped Seven Mile Pond.

By **Mile 33** you're back in the Alpena city limits. Turn right (south) on Chisholm Street (US-23), where you will cross the Thunder Bay River and backtrack to downtown Alpena. You'll pass the Cracker Barrel Party Store before you reach the marina parking lot At **Mile 35**. Past the downtown area on your left is Glen's Market, open 24 hours. In the marina area there's a tourist information stand, the Deckside Deli and marine charter information.

Shorter option (7 miles) Alpena's new River Path is a network of eight-foot-wide bikes paths, paved shoulders and sidewalks. For an enjoyable 7-mile route start at Mich-e-ke-wis Park on the south end of the city limits just off US-23. The park includes picnic areas, 1/2 mile of sandy beach and the best swimming area in town.

Follow the paths and sidewalks into the downtown area where you can pick up the River Path at the Second Street bridge. From the south side of the river, you cross the bridge by Lamarre Park to continue on the path on the river's north side. Continue along the path by making a left on Chisholm Street to Island Park. The path passes by the Jesse Besser Museum and Alpena Community College.

Island Park (sorry, no restrooms) includes nature trails along a bluff where you can view the marshy river with its many islands and look for geese and ducks. The delightful park is actually an island that is crossed by a bridge from a parking area along US-23.

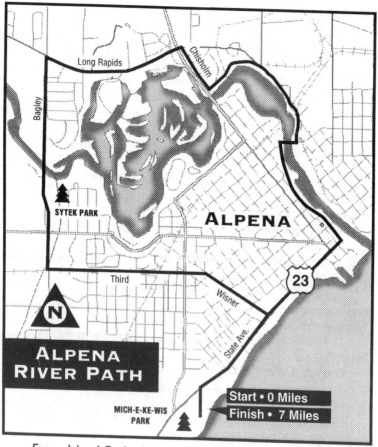

Long Rapids

Chisholm

Bagley

SYTEK PARK

ALPENA

23

Third

Wisner

State Ave.

N

**ALPENA
RIVER PATH**

MICH-E-KE-WIS
PARK

Start • 0 Miles
Finish • 7 Miles

From Island Park, there is a separate bike path along Long Rapids Road. Turn left (south) on Bagley and continue along its eight-foot-wide, paved shoulders to Third Street. Sytek Park is located just south of the Thunder Bay River on the east side of Bagley. The last portion of this route travels on residential roads. Turn left (east) on Third Street, right on Wisner Street and then right (south) on State Avenue (US-23) to return to Mich-e-ke-wis Park.

Bicycle sales, service

Cobblestone Cyclery, 225 W. Chisholm, Alpena; ☎ (517)

356-1238.

Summit Sports, 224 E. Chisholm, Alpena; ☎ (517) 356-1182.

Tour America Bike Shop, 268 N. 2nd, Rogers City; ☎ (517) 734-3946.

Area attractions

Jesse Besser Museum, Alpena; ☎ (517) 356-2202.

Dinosaur Gardens Prehistoric Zoo, Ossineke ☎ (517) 471-5477.

Presque Isle Lighthouse and Museum, Presque Isle; ☎ (517) 595-2787.

Sportsmen's Island and the Alpena Wildfowl Sanctuary (Island Park), Alpena.

Area festivals and events

June: Riverfest/Thunder Bay River Canoe Races, Alpena.

July: July 4th parade, Block Party, Michigan Brown Trout Festival, Port Huron to Alpena Sailboat Race, Art on the Bay; Ossineke Old Fashioned Days.

August: Ramblin' Rods Car Show, Antique Tractor and Steam Engine Show, Alpena County Fair, Alpena; Nautical Festival, Rogers City Salmon Tournament, Rogers City.

October: Fall Harvest Day, Cripp's Fruit Farm Fall Pumpkin Festival, Alpena.

Travel information

Thunder Bay Visitors Bureau; ☎ (800) 4-ALPENA or (517) 354-4181.

Michigan's Sunrise Side, 1361 Fletcher St., National City, MI 48748; ☎ (800) 424-3022.

Cycling Trip Tip #18

THE THREE MOST COMMON plACES wHERE TOURING cyclists cRASH is oN RAilROAd TRACKS, sEWER gRATES ANd loose gRAVEl shouldERS. WHEN APPROACHING RAilROAd TRACKS, alWAYS CROSS AT A 90-dEGREE ANglE OR dismouNT ANd walk.

28

Black Lake Tour

Trip Card

Starting point: Onaway State Park
County: Presque Isle
Distance: 34 miles
Shorter option: 12.2 miles
Terrain: flat, some rolling hills
Highlights: Ocqueoc Falls, Black Mountain
Forest Recreation Area
Suggested riders: intermediate

After the exodus of summer visitors but before the leaf peepers arrive for fall colors is the best time for cycling in northeast Michigan. Remotely quiet is the best description of the Black Lake region in late September when I cycled this 34 mile route.

The leaves hinted at the full palette of colors to come, the temperature hovered in the 60's and there was no one around. Nicely paved roads and rolling hills wind through the 158-acre Onaway State Park, beautifully forested with white and red pine, maple, oak and birch. Some of the 103 camp sites are located on Black Lake, a body of water more than 6 miles in length and 4 miles wide at its widest point.

This refreshing route winds along lightly traveled roads and past the woods and waters of the Black Mountain Forest Recreation Area. Handicapped accessible hiking trails, revamped cross country ski trails, three campgrounds and other recent changes have made the state forest recreation area an alluring destination to outdoor enthuisasts.

To add mileage or as a side trip, visit the Ocqueoc Falls, the most accessible waterfall in the Lower Peninsula, located 2 miles off Ocqueoc Road, 18.8 miles into this route.

As Black Lake is close to other well-known destinations like Mackinaw City, lot of visitors bypass the area on their way to somewhere else. And that's the way we like it!

To reach the area, depart I-75 at exit 310 and head east on M-68. Within 19 miles you arrive in the town of Onaway, then head north on M-211 which ends at Onaway State Park. You'll need either a daily vehicle permit or a annual state park pass to enter and park your car.

Stage one (12 miles) Start in the day-use area of Onaway State Park. Cycle out of the park on a beautiful, hilly asphalt road lined with tall northwoods trees. Just past the entrance to the state park turn left (east) on Bonz Beach Highway (County Road 489). You will pass a lakeside motel in the first mile after the road makes a sharp curve to the north.

County Road 489 is two lanes wide with gravel shoulders and little traffic. You'll have views of Black Lake before the road makes some sharp curves through sections of evergreens and tall hardwoods. Stay on County Road 489 as it curves to the right at **Mile 2.4**, while Black Mountain Road veers off to the left. You're in the beautiful Black Mountain Forest Recreation Area amd will soon pass a snowmobile trailhead at **Mile 4.4**. The road twists and curves following a downhill stretch at **Mile 5**.

Turn right (east) on Town Hall Highway (County Road 646) at **Mile 5.7**, which is a primarily flat but bumpy road with no shoulders. You stay in the woods for the most part until reaching US-23 at **Mile 11**. Turn right (southeast) on the state highway that has wide paved shoulders. If you're hungry, you can stop at a small store before crossing the Ocqueoc River at **Mile 12**.

Stage two (16 miles) Continuing on US-23, you'll cycle up a small hill before turning right (south) onto Ocqueoc Road which immediately goes uphill. Forested Ocqueoc Road is a wide, two-lane road ideal for cycling. You'll encounter the biggest uphill on this route at **Mile 14.4** just before the Trinity Lutheran Church, a scenic white country church. Another relatively large hill is climbed at **Mile 17.8** before passing North Allis Highway.

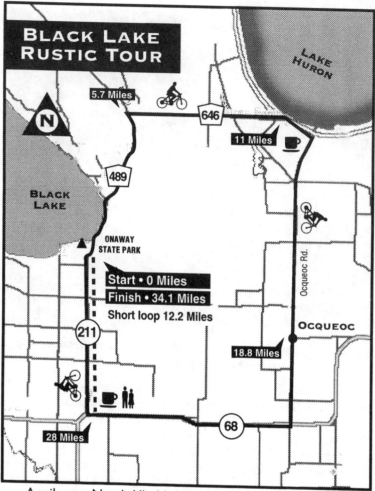

BLACK LAKE RUSTIC TOUR

N

5.7 Miles

646

11 Miles

489

BLACK LAKE

ONAWAY STATE PARK

Start • 0 Miles
Finish • 34.1 Miles
Short loop 12.2 Miles

211

Ocqueoc Rd.

OCQUEOC

18.8 Miles

28 Miles

68

A mile past North Allis Highway is the junction with Ocqueoc Falls Highway where you turn left (east) for the 2-mile side trip to the cascade. The falls is located in a day-use area on the north side of the road and includes picnic tables, vault toilets and the Ocqueoc Falls Pathway, a hiking trail of 3, 5 and 6-mile loops.

To see the falls themselves, however, you need only to walk about 50 yards from the parking area. The claim of Ocqueoc Falls used to be the "only waterfall in the Lower Peninsula" but a small cascade has since been discovered just off the Manistee River on

Ocqueoc Falls, only one of two waterfalls in the Lower Peninsula, makes for a pleasant stop on the Black Lake Tour.

the west side of the state. Ocqueoc is still the most visited falls south of the Mackinac Bridge and a beautiful spot for an extended break. The waterfall is actually a series of ledges where the Ocqueoc River drops about six feet.

Back on the main route, Ocqueoc Road continues south into Case Township, where there is a series of rolling hills, before arriving at a stop sign at M-68 at *Mile 21.5*. Turn right (west) on M-68, which can be busier than the other roads on this route. On the way to Onaway, the state highway runs through rolling farm fields, passes a classic red barn and crosses the Black River at *Mile 25.4*. You climb a long but gradual hill and then enter Onaway, the Sturgeon Capital of Michigan, at *Mile 28*.

Onaway, with a population of just over 1,000 residents, is an inviting, homey town. American flags greeted us on a late September afternoon. For food there's an IGA grocery store, Carter's Food Store and a Dairy Queen on M-68.

Stage three (6 miles) Just past the Onaway Outdoor Sports store is M-211 (Main Street in town) where you want to turn right (north) to return to Onaway State Park. This road is bumpy in spots and features gravel shoulders. Just before the entrance to the state park there's a pizza parlor and a party store. Cross Bonz Beach Highway and venture back into the park.

You'll certainly enjoy the forested state park road back to the parking area as you climb a small hill to reach the day-use area at **Mile 34.** Within the day-use area there are picnic tables, a shelter, drinking water, bathrooms and even a small beach on the lake.

Shorter option: Onaway State Park to Onaway and back makes a nice 12-mile option for campers or park visitors who want a shorter distance.

Bicycle sales, service
Cobblestone Cyclery, 225 W. Chisholm, Alpena; ☎ (517) 356-1238.

Summit Sports, 224 E. Chisholm, Alpena; ☎ (517) 356-1182.

Sheldon's Cycle Center, 123 E. State, Cheboygan; ☎ (616) 627-9366.

Wheels 'N Motion, 209 W. State St., Cheboygan; ☎ (616) 627-3321.

Tour America Bike Shop, 268 N. Second, Rogers City; ☎ (517) 734-3946.

Area attractions
Presque Isle Lighthouse and Museum, Presque Isle; ☎ (517) 595-2787.

Area events and festivals
August: Nautical Festival, Rogers City.
September: Posen Potato Festival, Posen.

Travel information
Michigan's Sunrise Side, 1361 Fletcher St., National City, MI 48748; ☎ (800) 424-3022.

Rogers City Visitors Bureau; ☎ (800) 622-4148.

Onaway Area Chamber of Commerce; ☎ (517) 733-2874.

Onaway State Park; ☎ (517) 733-8279.

The lumber mill at Mill Creek State Park is explained to visitors at the historic park.

29

Mackinaw Shoreline

Trip Card

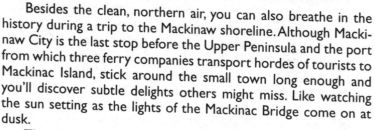

Starting Point: Mackinaw City
Counties: Emmet, Cheboyban
Distance: 50 miles
Shorter option: 7 miles
Terrain: Flat
Highlights: Mackinaw City, Lake Huron shoreline, Cheboygan, Wilderness State Park
Suggested riders: intermediate

Besides the clean, northern air, you can also breathe in the history during a trip to the Mackinaw shoreline. Although Mackinaw City is the last stop before the Upper Peninsula and the port from which three ferry companies transport hordes of tourists to Mackinac Island, stick around the small town long enough and you'll discover subtle delights others might miss. Like watching the sun setting as the lights of the Mackinac Bridge come on at dusk.

There's something special about being at the tip of Michigan's Lower Peninsula; a strong Indian heritage, a strategic location where lakes Huron and Michigan come together, and the beautiful scenery of the northwoods, beaches and inland lakes make it a prime destination for cyclists. The majestic Mackinac Bridge looms as a backdrop in many spots when cycling in this area. The "Mighty Mac", as it's often called, is the only link between the Lower and Upper peninsulas and is the third longest bridge in the country. A trip across the bridge provides a panorama of shorelines, Great Lakes and islands galore along with ferries, freighters and fishing boats. Twice a year, cyclists can cross the "Mighty Mac" as part of the Scenic Shoreline Bike Tour in June and September.

Our route begins in Mackinaw City, with all its attractions, food choices and scenery. It veers east on US-23, a wide road with nicely paved shoulders. Tantalizing glimpses of Lake Huron and a mixture of trees, woods, cabins and campgrounds make up this stretch of the route as you venture into Cheboygan and back to Mackinaw City via the back roads.

Cheboygan, a Lake Huron town of 5,100, is known for its 40-mile Inland Waterway and an old-time jail at the Cheboygan County Historical Museum. The town also offers cyclists an array of places to eat. You can also visit Cheboygan State Park, a peninsula surrounded by three bodies of water: to the north is the South Channel of the Straits of Mackinac, to the west is Duncan Bay, and to the east, Lake Huron.

Back in Mackinaw City, you can learn more about the Indian culture at Teysen's Woodland Indian Museum, above the family restaurant on Huron Street. There are displays of tools, clothing, food and art of the Woodland Indian culture. At Colonial Michilimackinac, a reconstructed fur-trading village, you can watch archaeologists excavate ruins at the longest on-going archaeological dig in the country, view a colonial wedding re-enactment, or watch the daily arrival of voyageurs.

Because of Mackinaw City's fudge shops, Colonial Michilimackinac State Park, Mill Creek State Park, and numerous festivals and special events, "Making It Mackinaw" (Mackinaw Area Tourist Bureau's motto) isn't a hard decision.

Stage one (3.5 miles) The route begins on Huron Street at the Mackinaw Area Tourist Bureau, across from the Star Line Ferry. Heading south, you'll pass a strip of hotels and restaurants including the Ramada Inn and Embers Restaurant. Veer to the left following the lakeshore to stay on US-23. (The East Route of the League of Michigan Bicyclists' 7-day Shoreline Bicycle Tour uses US-23 from Cheboygan to Mackinaw City as a leg of its tour.) This road features wide, paved shoulders most of the way to Cheboygan. You'll pass many more motels including the Chippewa Motor Lodge, North Star Motel and Knights Inn.

At **Mile 1.2** you're out of Mackinaw City, heading toward

N

**MACKINAW
SHORELINE**

CHEBOYGAN

15.7 Miles

23

Mackinaw Ave.

Levering Rd.

MILL CREEK STATE
HISTORICAL PARK

MACKINAW CITY
Start • 0 Miles
Finish • 50 Miles
Short loop 15 Miles

Central Ave.

Levering Rd.

45.5 Miles

Wilderness Park Dr.

Bay Rd.

Gill Rd.

**CARP
LAKE**

Reed Rd.

36.2 Miles

32 Miles

Cheboygan. There are some prime northwoods trees and a couple of commerical campgrounds along the way. Mackinaw Mill Creek Camping, passed at **Mile 2.7**, includes a heated pool and views of the Mackinac Bridge and Lake Huron.

Mill Creek State Historical Park is reached at **Mile 3.5**. You can take an early break (or come back later) and wander through this historic attraction. In the 1780's a Scottish trader named Robert Campbell purchased the 640-acre tract of land, built a 10-foot cedar dam and constructed an ingenious sawmill, powered by Mill Creek, proving that one man and an ox could cut 15-20 times more planks than the best pitman-top sawyer in the region.

In 1984, a working duplicate of the 1790 water-powered sawmill was built below the mill dam. Hourly demonstrations are given to show how a system of wheels and gears used water power to cut the huge logs into planks. The park also has 1.5 miles of nature trails including a half-mile walk that borders the creek and passes two scenic overlooks with views of the Straits and Mackinac Island.

Stage two (12.2 miles) Cycle onward! As you ride along US-23, a predominantly flat road that's good for picking up speed, you'll enjoy some great views of Lake Huron. A stand of pine is reached at **Mile 7**, followed by a campground and a small roadside park with picnic tables within a half mile.

After you pass the Two Mile Inn (noted for its homemade pizza bar) you'll know you're approaching civilization by the increasing number of homes. The Cheboygan city limits sign is reached near **Mile 14**. Use caution as the road makes a curve into town where there's a mixture of businesses and motels. Of interest to some cyclists may be the Earth Gallery Gifts on your right or the Yeck Family Drive-in to your left at **Mile 14.7**. The road is now called Mackinaw Street. You will cycle to the right toward US-23 in town where you'll reach the downtown area at **Mile 15.7**.

In town there's a vast array of food choices; you'll find everything from Dairy Queen and Big Boy to Arbie's, McDonalds and Pizza Hut. Locals recommend Mickey's Mini Mart at 1203 South Main Street for its deli, This Old House at 112 Jackson St. for its pizza, subs and sandwiches, and the Carnation on 423 Main Street for inexpensive, yet good dining.

Cyclists cross Mackinac Bridge during an annual weekend bicycle event in Mackinaw City.

Stage three (20.5 miles) From downtown Cheboygan cycle west on State Street (later becomes Levering Road), which curves as you make your way out of town. This road is wide with some shoulders and sidewalks, but narrows to two lanes with gravel shoulders at **Mile 16.7**. You'll pass the Cheboygan City/ County Airport on your right at **Mile 19.2** as you pass through open country, residential and farm areas. The mostly flat road twists and curves beginning at **Mile 21.4**. After you've crested a hill you can look down and see far off into the distance. State Street becomes Levering Road after you pass a gas station at the I-75 interchange. Along Levering there's a mixture of gravel shoulders and paved shoulders. A gradual downhill stretch is reached at **Mile 30** before the road makes a curve to your right. Just past Paradise Lake Road you will cross from Cheboygan into Emmet County.

Make a quick right (north) onto US-31 and then a left onto

West Levering Road. At **Mile 31.5**, where there's a sign pointing to Cross Village, the road is a bit bumpy with no shoulders. You'll cycle through a residential section and small rolling hills but don't despair; you won't have to go up that huge hill you see straight ahead. Turn right (north) onto Reed Road before the hill at **Mile 32**. This is a scenic road where lilacs bloom and country fences grace the fields. You'll climb a big hill near **Mile 33** and then pass Schmalzried Road. Reed Road, a scenic pedal through many wooded areas, has no shoulders but also very light traffic.

Stage four (13.3 miles) Turn left (west) onto Gill Road at **Mile 36.2**. This road is partially lined with birch trees and is a bit bumpy here with no shoulders and usually light traffic. After you make your way up a long, gradual uphill, Gill Road flattens out with a nice straightaway beginning at **Mile 37.7**. Turn right (north) onto Cecil Bay Road at **Mile 38.2**.

You'll pass the Wilderness Golf Course and a winding creek before the road curves left (west) into Wilderness State Park. Wilderness Park Drive is a tree-lined road through the state park and for cyclists a beautiful journey through an unspoiled natural area. You can either turn right (east) onto Wilderness Park Drive to return to Mackinaw City, or left (west) to venture further into the state park (one of the largest in the Lower Peninsula).

Thirty miles of shoreline grace this 7,514-acre unit, as well as a natural area and a vast network of trails through a forest of pines and hardwoods. The park has 210 modern campsites divided among two campgrounds. There are also five trailside cabins and three 24-bunk lodges for rent.

Near Cecil Bay outside of the park, Wilderness Park Drive becomes County Road 81 but remains lightly traveled. It twists and turns as you head east on it back to Mackinaw City, past wildflowers in the summer and incredible views of the Mackinac Bridge whenever the weather its clear. The road winds through a nice shoreline stretch at **Mile 44** where it's important to watch out for hidden drives and pedestrian signs. You make a sharp curve to your right at the base of a gradual hill and then at **Mile 45.5** turn left (north) to continue to follow County Road 81.

When the road ends, make a sharp right onto West Central Avenue (still part of County Road 81), which has paved shoulders

Cycling past Lake Huron is a highlight of many tours in East Michigan, including the Mackinaw Shoreline tour.

on both sides. You'll pass the Mackinaw City Public Schools on your right (the starting point for the Big Mac Shoreline organized tour in June and September) before reaching a strip of motels, inns and shops.

No doubt hungry cyclists will notice a Dairy Queen and a TCBY Yogurt in the business district. There's the internationally acclaimed Marshall's Fudge on your right at **Mile 49** as well as T-shirt shops and restaurants. Turn right onto Huron Street where you'll pass the Putt-Putt Treasure Island Challenge Golf and the Traverse Bay Woolen Company - a log cabin shop with plenty of sweaters, afghans, flannel shirts and other favorites of outdoor enthusiasts. Before you reach the Mackinaw Area Tourist Bureau near **Mile 50**, you'll pass the St. Julian retail outlet, more motels, Alice's Candy Corn and the Mackinaw Pastie and Cookie Co.

Time to lock up the bikes, gather your non-cycling companions and figure out your itinerary for the rest of your visit to the Mackinaw area.

Shorter option (7 miles) Traveling Huron Street in Mackinaw City to M-23 to Mill Creek State Historical Park and back offers beginners a nice option and a visit to one of the most popular attractions.

Bicycle sales, service
Balsam Sports, 20 N. State St., St. Ignace, ☎ (906) 643-6395.
Area attractions
Colonial Michilimackinac, Mackinaw City, ☎ (616) 436-5563.
Mill Creek State Park, Mackinaw City, ☎ (616) 436-7301.
Teysen's Indian Museum, Mackinaw City, ☎ (616) 436-7011.
Cheboygan Victorian Opera House, ☎ (616) 627-5841.
Cheboygan Historical Museum, ☎ (616) 627-9597.
Area events, festivals
May: Fort Michilimackinac Pageant and Parade.
June: Soap Opera Fan Fair, Big Mac Scenic Shoreline Bike Ride, Ride Across the Mighty Mac, Kite Festival, Jog Across the Mighty Mac, Mackinaw City Fudge Classic, Mackinaw City; Cheboygan Street Rod Car Show, Cheboygan.
July: Independence Day Waterfront Events and Fireworks, Velvet Moon of Mackinaw Trade Fair and Rendezvous, Mackinaw City; Bliss Festival, Bliss.
August: Antique Show, Ironworkers Festival, Annual Corvette Show, Art Fair, Mackinaw City; Northern Michigan Fair, Cheboygan.
September: Annual Labor Day Bridge Walk, Scenic Shoreline Fall Bike Tour, Bike Across the Mighty Mac, Mackinaw City.
October: Fall Shoppers Festival, Mackinaw City.
Travel information
Mackinaw Area Tourist Bureau; ☎ (800) 666-0160 or (616) 436-5664.
Mackinaw City Chamber of Commerce; ☎ (616) 436-5574.
Cheboygan Chamber of Commerce; ☎ (616) 627-7183.
Wilderness State Park; ☎ (616) 436-5381.
Cheboygan State Park; ☎ (616) 627-2811.

30

Magical Mackinac

Trip Card

Starting point: Downtown area
of Mackinac Island
County: Mackinac
Distance: 8.1 miles
Shorter option: 2.5 miles
Terrain: Flat, paved road
Highlights: Scenic views of Lake Huron,
historical sights, Fort Mackinac
Suggested Riders: Beginner

The magic of Mackinac? What could be more magical for cyclists than an island without cars?

Or a place steeped in history, attractions, charming hotels and bed and breakfasts, spectacular scenery at almost every curve in the road, an unlimited supply of fudge...but no motorized traffic, not even if it's 5 p.m. and everybody is going home.

The magic of Mackinac? For cyclists it's M-185, the only state road in Michigan where they ride down the middle and only have to worry about horses and carriages.

Hard-core cyclists, looking for the challenge of a 50-mile ride, will pass up this historic island. M-185 is an 8.1-mile loop and even if you add British Landing Road or other roads that cut across the middle of the island, it's impossible to put together a tour of more than 15 miles.

But whether you're seriously training or not, Mackinac Island is still a mecca for cyclists. It's not the mileage that attracts people with a bike in tow, but the opportunity of riding from one scenic limestone formation and historic site to the next. You may not be able to add 40 miles to the odometer but you can easily spend a day pedalling M-185 with stops at rocks known as Devil's Kitchen and Lover's Leap, the nature center at British Landing and, of course, Michigan's most famous fort. With cannons on display, horses trotting along next to you and fudge shops, Mackinac is, and probably always will be, the premier bike ride for families.

If you are turned off by the crush of tourists at the height of the summer season, consider staying overnight on the island. The real magic of Mackinac happens at 5 p.m. after most of the day visitors head back to the mainland and a quiet, almost intriguing atmosphere descends on the Island and the people who live there.

Or consider a trip in the off-season, especially September or October when the fall colors are brilliant, the fudge shops are closed and the roads empty of horses, in-line skaters and other cyclists.

Getting There: Three ferry companies service the island from both Mackinaw City in the Lower Peninsula and St. Ignace in the Upper Peninsula . Boats run from late April to early November and occasionally even later with more than 100 trips daily during the peak of the season. The fares are the same for all three and all of them will carry your bicycle. Call Star Line (☎ 800-638-9892), Shepler's Mackinac Island Ferry (☎ 800-828-6157) or Arnold Transit Company (☎ 800-542-8528).

Stage One (3.6 miles) No matter what ferry you choose or what town you depart from, you will end up in what is commonly referred to as the "downtown area" of Mackinac Island where Huron Street serves as main street. You literally step off the boat into the Victorian charm of Mackinac that during the summer is bustling with draft horses, carriages and what seem to be thousands of cyclists. If you didn't bring a bicycle, rental shops and their two-wheeled wares will be along on Huron Street. So will the fudge shops.

Head west on Huron, past the Lilac Tree Hotel and the Windermere Hotel, and quickly the street becomes Lake Shore Road (M-185) and begins skirting Lake Huron. Once you pass the Mackinac Island school, you'll be free of that maddening downtown crowd.

M-185 is paved and features both mileage markers along the

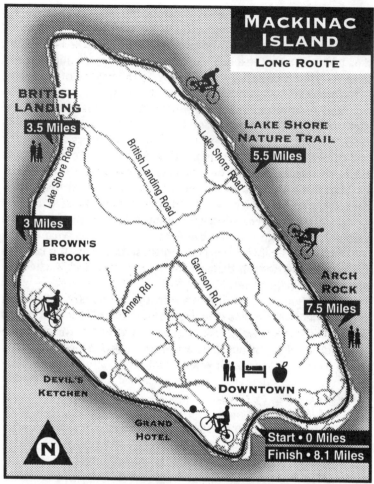

MACKINAC ISLAND
LONG ROUTE

BRITISH LANDING
3.5 Miles

LAKE SHORE NATURE TRAIL
5.5 Miles

Lake Shore Road

British Landing Road

Lake Shore Road

3 Miles

BROWN'S BROOK

Garrison Rd.

Annex Rd.

ARCH ROCK
7.5 Miles

DEVIL'S KETCHEN

DOWNTOWN

GRAND HOTEL

Start • 0 Miles
Finish • 8.1 Miles

N

way and benches (bicyclist's rest areas?). The views of the water here and the great spans of the Mackinac Bridge in the distance are spectacular. Within 1.5 miles of the downtown area, you arrive at Devil's Kitchen, a group of limestone sea caves, niches really, that were formed 350 million years ago. Most visitors stop here to admire the panorama of the bridge and the northern tip of the Lower Peninsula. Nearby is Lover's Leap, a limestone pillar that rises 145 feet above Lake Huron. Interpretive displays explain both formations.

You continue up the west shore of the Island and at **Mile 3** you round Heriot Point and arrive at Brown's Brook. The natural spring tumbles out of a stand of cedar and into Lake Huron as a small stream. It can be a quiet and cool spot on a hot summer day. Nearby is another interpretive display on the wildlife of the Island.

The next stop is British Landing, the only junction along M-185 and reached 3.5 miles from downtown. It was here on the night of July 16, 1812 that Capt. Charles Roberts arrived with 35 British regulars and hundreds of voyageur paddlers and Indians and then slipped across the island to the hill above Fort Mackinac. From this vantage point he was able to capture Fort Mackinac without firing a shot at the Americans. Two years later the Americans tried to recapture the island by using the same trick. The British, however, were waiting in ambush just up the road from British Landing and crushed the American forces at what is now Wawashkamo Golf Course. The route used to cross the island is British Landing Road. It departs south from here and reaches the historic fort in 2.5 miles.

At the junction, you'll find a refreshment stand open during the summer, picnic tables, drinking water and the "Last Restrooms Before The City" as well as cannons on display and historical markers. The Mackinac Island Nature Center is also located here and inside has a few displays on wildlife and other natural topics. During the summer the nature center staff lead a number of guided walks on the nearby trails.

Stage Two (4.5 miles) M-185 continues north and continues to hug the shoreline. In a little over a half mile from British Landing, you pass Point Aux Pins, the northernmost point of the island. From here you can see the shoreline of the Upper Peninsula both to the north and to the west.

Once past Point Aux Pins, M-185 begins curving south for the return journey to the downtown area. At **Mile 5.5** you reach the Lake Shore Nature Trail where there are benches and bike racks. The short trail takes you around a small pond that in early summer is loaded with wildflowers including Indian paintbrush, striped coral root and even the endangered yellow lady slipper.

You continue south along M-185 and at **Mile 7.5** arrive at the Island's most stunning rock formation high above you - Arch Rock.

Checking out Devil's Kitchen on Mackinac Island.

There are benches and bike racks here and from the road it is a steep climb of 192 steps to reach the top. But the view of Lake Huron through the arch is worth the knee-bending climb. Besides, there are restrooms up there.

Indians believed Arch Rock was formed by giant fairies, who used the formation as a gateway to the island. Early writers often compared it with Virginia's "Natural Bridge." Today it's the main reason to venture beyond the fudge shops on Main Street.

The formation stands 150 feet above Lake Huron and is almost a perfect 50-foot-wide arch. It was created 4000 years ago when the higher levels of the Great Lake dissolved the softer

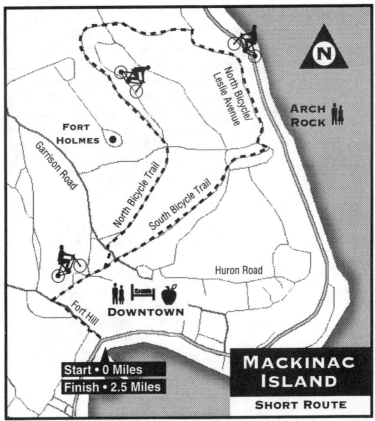

materials of what was then a bluff. As the lake eroded the base, the soft rock in the middle crumbled into the water, leaving the firm Breccia limestone arch standing.

Once you return to your bike, it's only a half mile until you pass the sprawling Mission Point Resort complex and re-enter the downtown area of the Island. Want to add a few more miles to the tour? Continue onto the shorter option that follows to see more caves, rock formations and the view from Fort Holmes.

Shorter Option (2.5 miles) The North and South Bike Path on Mackinac Island can be combined to form a 2.5-mile loop from the downtown area. If you have young children, keep in mind it begins with a very steep climb up Fort Hill Road past the entrance to Fort Mackinac to the Governor's Summer Residence.

At this point head east along Huron Road past the limestone walls and blockhouses of Fort Mackinac and then pick up the South Bicycle Trail. Within a half mile of the fort you reach Arch Rock where you encounter the North Bike Path. This paved path dips and winds along the shoreline bluff, providing views of the Great Lake below before swinging inland and passing Sugar Loaf, a 30-foot high limestone stack that looks like it belongs in a desert out west. Don't pass up the climb to Fort Holmes where the British once set up a six-pound cannon and re-claimed the fort from the Americans in 1812 without firing a shot. The view is stunning.

Bicycle sales, service

Balsam Sports, Huron St., Mackinac Island; ☎ (906) 847-6335.

Orr-Kid's Bicycles, Huron St., Mackinac Island; ☎ (906) 847-3211.

Bicycle Rentals

Island Bicycle Rental, Huron St., Mackinac Island; ☎ (906) 847-6288.

Ryba's Bike Rental, Huron St., Mackinac Island; ☎ (906) 847-3384.

Lakeside Streetside Bike Rentals, Huron St., Mackinac Island; ☎ (906) 847-3351 or 847-6350.

Area Attractions

Fort Mackinac and Mackinac Island State Park; ☎ (906) 847-6330.

Jack's Livery Stable, Mahoney Ave., Mackinac Island; ☎ (906) 847-3391.

Cindy's Riding Stables, Market St., Mackinac Island; ☎ (906) 847-3572.

Area events and festivals

June: Lilac Festival

July: Stone Skipping Contest; Chicago-To-Mackinac Yacht Race; Port Huron-To-Mackinac Island Yacht Race.

September: Labor Day Mackinac Bridge Walk, St. Ignace.

Travel information

Mackinac Island Chamber of Commerce, ☎ (906) 847-6418.

Mackinac Island State Parks, ☎ (906) 847-3328.

Participants prepare for an organized bike tour in Shiawassee and Saginaw Counties.

Appendix

East Michigan Cycling Clubs

Adrian Maple Wheelers, P.O. Box 895, Adrian MI 49221-0895; ☎ (517)423-1223.

Albion Bicycle Club, 25031 D Drive, Homer MI 49425.

Ann Arbor Bicycle & Touring Society, P.O. Box 1585, Ann Arbor, MI 48106-1585; ☎ (313) 337-5050.

Cadieux Bicycle Club, 37817 Greenwich Dr., Mount Clemens, MI 48043; ☎ (313) 463-7222.

Cascades Cycling Club, P.O. Box 515, Jackson, MI 49204-0515; ☎ (517) 782-3288.

Clinton River Riders, 36558 Moravian Dr., Clinton Township, MI 48035; ☎ (313) 752-6310.

Cycling Saddlemen Bicycling Club, P.O. Box 2449, Dearborn, MI 48123-2449; ☎ (313) 278-1350.

Downriver Cycling Club, P.O. Box 488, Flat Rock, MI 48134-0488; ☎ (313) 675-0419.

Ford Cycling Club, 7215 Belleville, Belleville, MI 48111-1183; ☎ (313) 699-6925.

Flying Rhino Bicycle Club, 60 S. Main St., Clarkston, MI 48346; ☎ (810) 625-7000.

Genesee Wanderers Bicycle Club, P.O. Box 801 Flint, MI 4850; ☎ (810) 732-2079.

Monroe County Cycling, 474 Lavender, Monroe, MI 48161.

Slow Spokes of Macomb County, P.O. Box 3015, Center Line, MI 48015-0015.

Tri-County Bicycle Association, 2693 Frank St., Lansing,

MI 48911-6402; ☎ (517) 882-8291.

    Tri-City Cyclists Club, P.O. Box 2156, Bay City, MI 48707-2156; ☎ (517) 892-2100.

    Westland Cycling Club, P.O. Box 786, Westland, MI 48185.

    Wolverine Sports Club, P.O. Box 63 Royal Oak, MI 48067; ☎ (313) 547-0050

Annual rides in East Michigan

    May: *Clean Air Challenge*, Milford; *Metro Grand Spring Tour*, New Boston; *Southeast Michigan Warm-up Ride*, Canton; *Back 40 Challenge*, Clarkston; *Lapeer County Warm-up Magic Ride*, Lapeer; *Frankenmuth Fahrrad Tour*, Frankenmuth; *Detroit Receiving/Wolverine 200*, Detroit; *Maple City Metric*, Adrian; *Genesee County Warm-up Magic Ride*, Clio.

    June: *100,000 Meter T-Shirt Ride*, Grand Ledge; *Michigan Human Powered Vehicle Rally*, Waterford; *Captain Aluminum Invitational*, Washington; *Farm Lake Tour*, Plymouth; *Shoreline Scenic Bike Tour & Ride Across the Mackinac Bridge*, Mackinaw City; *Magic Ride Bicycle Tour*, Holt; *Thumbs Up Bicycle Tour*, Port Austin; *Pedal for PUPS*, Elsie; *Pedal Across Lower Michigan*, Ann Arbor; *Ride of Note*, Corunna.

    July: *Liberty Tour*, Bay City; *Firecracker 100 Bicycle Tour*, Brighton; *Women on Wheels*, Mason; *MS 150 Bike Tour*, Livonia; *Summer Tour Week-End*, DeWitt; *Summer Tour V*, DeWitt; *One Helluva Ride*, Chelsea; *Detroit Free Press Michigander*, Lansing; *Tour of the Thumb*, St. Clair; *Shoreline Bicycle Tour East*, AuGres; *Minard Mills Bicycle Tour & Wienie Roast*, Jackson.

    August: *Assenmacher 100*, Swartz Creek; *The Jac Ride*, Jackson; *Chelsea Challenge Bike for Burns*, Chelsea; *Al's Fund Raiser*, St. Clair; *Dalmac*, Lansing.

Among the many great eateries in East Michigan is Zingerman's Delicatessen in Ann Arbor. The deli is a long time favorite of both cyclists and University of Michigan students. (photo by Ken Bawcom)

September: *The Triple Trail Challenge,* Pinckney; *One Day Ride Across Michigan (ODRAM),* Muskegon; *Fall Family Fun Ride,* New Boston; *A Peach of a Ride,* Armada; *Fall Shoreline Scenic Bike Tour & Ride Across the Mackinac Bridge,* Mackinaw City; *MS Fall Breakaway Bike Tour,* Kensington Metro Park, Milford; *Harvest Tour,* Lapeer; *Celebration of Cycling,* Livonia.

October: *Friends of the Rouge Pedal Fest,* Westland; *Blue Water Ramble,* St. Clair; *Back 40 Challenge,* Clarkston; *Famous Falling Leaves Forty or Fifty,* Saline.

January: *First Dozen Ride,* Dearborn; *Polar Rhino Ride,* Clarkston.

The Author

Karen Gentry, a resident of Grand Rapids, Mich., is an information specialist for Kent County. She formerly worked as a reporter and for the West Michigan Tourist Association where she was the project coordinator for the first Lake Michigan Circle Tour Guide.

A journalism graduate of Central Michigan University, Gentry is also frequent contributor of bicycling articles to various magazines and newspapers and author of *Cycling Michigan: Twenty-five of the Best Routes in Western Michigan* (Pegg Legg Publications). This is her second book.